"Written in a truly conversational style, Dr. Tsao harnesses decades of patient care with his untraditional look at traditional psychiatric tenants. His thoughtful insights offer the public a truly rare glimpse into the therapeutic process and the mind of a psychiatrist. A must and provocative read to say the least, especially Dr. Tsao's somewhat unconventional although entertaining take on human sexuality. There's definitely something for everyone who reads Tsaoism"

David W. Goodman, M.D.
Assistant Professor of Psychiatry and
Behavioral Science
Johns Hopkins School of Medicine

"This book is Freud translated for the rest of us in today's language. Dr. Tsao has taken insights from psychoanalysis and woven them in with other schools of thought and the latest concepts of neurobiology and genetics to present an understanding of human behavior that makes understandable common sense, not a small accomplishment indeed. His narratives about the lives of some of his patients make the book engaging, entertaining and alive. His unique conversational style leaves the impression that this is a discussion between old friends. A really enjoyable and quick read that I would strongly recommend to everyone from layman to the most sophisticated professional"

Michael J. Manos, Ph.D.
Clinical Psychologist
Center Head, Pediatric Behavioral Health
Cleveland Clinic

TSAOISM

BY DR. TOM TSAO

Published in the United States by
KoehlerBooks.com

Library of Congress Cataloging and Publication Data
Tsao, Tom - 1941 -
Tsaoism

ISBN 0-9765932-4-6

Printed by Quad Graphics
September, 2010

For more information about this book and all other inquiries,
please Email: tsaoism@koehlerbooks.com

Edited by Tia Stauffer
Cover and inside illustrations by Mary Britt
Back cover photo by James Harvey
Cover design by John Köehler

Contents

Introduction

Tsaoism is not a work about some new Eastern religion nor is it about some New Age personal philosophy. However, it is about human behavior and why human beings behave so predictably. It is not meant to be some self-help manual, but it might be that, particularly if you have children to raise. It is essentially Psychiatry 101 made simple and understandable for the average, normal person, whatever "normal" may be. It is meant for professionals and non-professionals alike. It is a peek into the secret sex lives of women and men plus a clear, scientific explanation of the painful male condition "blue balls." If this hasn't piqued your curiosity or interest, then I don't know what will.

Dr. Tsao

Tsaoism

by Dr. Tom Tsao

11/03/10

To Perla

Enjoy !!

DuT

1

Crazy Baby

One of my major objectives in taking on this literary endeavor was the realization that most people's lives are like the leaves of trees in the fall. After changing from green to various colors and shades thereof, the leaf falls off the tree and, with the autumn rain, is washed into a stream. The stream grows and flows, eventually emptying into a river downstream, in the process sweeping along the leaf. The river finds its way to the bay and finally into the ocean, where for the leaf and all its kindred souls the journey ends. Similarly, every person's life follows such a course from beginning to end. We, like the leaves, are swept along by the flow of life; we seldom or never swim against the current, passively being moved steadily toward the end of our solitary journey through life. To put it another way, as a friend recently told me, "Only the dead fish go with the flow." So, if your heart's still beating, swim against the current!

A U.S. Census study conducted over a half a century ago reported that the vast majority of Americans are born, live, die, and are buried within a one hundred-mile radius. It is my hope that reading this book will enlighten you and even inspire you to make waves, to swim against the current, to make conscious choices, to resist what others would call fate or predestination, to escape our predicted one hundred-mile radius fate.

With self-understanding of the psychological forces that drive your emotions and behavior, you may be free to make the changes that will take you into uncharted waters and give you the opportunity to live a richer, more self-determined, fulfilling, and meaningful life. Barring even the smallest self-change, at the very least you may be able to offer choice to your own children, or the next generation. Obviously, I'm not guaranteeing or implying that there are any easy solutions or "quick fixes" in this written conversation. Whatever there is to be discovered will be up to you, my readers.

In addition, if the life-changing and personality-molding events of each person's life can be identified and understood, it may help those people contemplating therapy or those already engaged in therapeutic work to move forward in a more timely manner toward a more positive, meaningful, and fulfilling outcome.

So, with more than forty-two years as a practicing physician and psychiatrist, I present for your consideration some of my observations and thoughts after logging more than 100,000 hours of therapeutic experience with people and sharing some of the more intimate aspects in the lives of more than 21,000 of my patients.

It seems logical to begin at the beginning and end at the end, as the Walrus said to Alice during her sojourn through Wonderland. Early in my career I sometimes felt like Alice, lost and confused as to why and when certain behaviors or emotions emerged in so many of the people who allowed me to delve into their most personal psychological lives.

As has been elucidated in the twenty-first century through the completion of the Human Genome Project, human beings receive from their parents about 40,000 genes of which 10,000 have some identifiable function that we know of at this time. We receive all these genes in the form of forty-six double-helix chromosomes, twenty-two pairs of autosomes and two sex chromosomes. The XX combination confirms femaleness and the XY maleness.

It is not my intent to bore you with scientific data or jargon. However, it is important to acknowledge that as Sigmund Freud predicted before his death in 1939, most of what were and are currently referred to as psychiatric disorders or syndromes will eventually be found to have a medical, biological, or genetic underpinning. Even as we establish the genetic roots of syndromes like Schizophrenia, Bipolar Disorder, Depression, Anxiety, and ADHD, and the differences that have been found in brain functioning, size, and anatomical topography in many of these maladies using X-ray, functional MRIs, SPECT, PET, and similar sophisticated technology, each person suffering with any one of these diagnoses is in fact unique. This then is the area I would like to explore with you—the uniqueness of each person. Logically, uniqueness is related to the almost limitless tapestry of human experience throughout the developmental and maturational process superimposed on our genetic heritage, half from mom and half from dad.

Over the past several decades, there have been many hypotheses promulgated about prenatal, perinatal, and immediate postnatal environments and their supposed long-term psychological impact on all of us. It has been suggested that the mother working or not working during pregnancy is of importance, that soft music and soft lighting in the delivery room have significant impact, that even the paint scheme of the hospital nursery is important. Not to say that some or all of these things may be important or not, but many of these beliefs or hypotheses have come and gone without any significant impact on the incidence of emotional disorders. On the other hand, things like alcohol consumption, tobacco and drug use and abuse, prematurity, and C-section delivery have been established to potentially lead to eventual negative outcomes in childhood and later adult behaviors.

So, let's take the Walrus's advice and start at the beginning with the birth of the baby. As I have explained over the years to my residents, interns, and medical students, by psychiatric definition, all babies are "crazy" or "psychotic"! That means they are totally out of touch with reality. Their reality is timeless and without boundaries or reason. Although skeptics will point out that infants of the human species are the most helpless of all newborns—and that fact is undoubtedly physiologically true—all of us who have had or have been involved with the caretaking of infants know the "real" truth of who is really in charge: the baby, of course! The crazy baby in his or her perception of the universe is at the absolute epicenter of it all, and the rest of us are just minions who serve the baby's every narcissistic, egocentric need. It is really magical from the infant's perspective! If the baby feels hungry, it's fed; if uncomfortable with a wet or poopy diaper, it's changed; if gassy, it's burped; if lonely, it's held, cuddled, or rocked—and all this without saying a single word, not that infants can actually talk anyway. A baby's all-powerful "thoughts" manipulate and control all in his or her world. Perish the thought that this being should express displeasure using a displeased countenance or vocalization! With the slightest verbal expression of frustration accompanied by anything from a small whimper to extreme wailing, its servants run helter-skelter to find what, if anything, will appease or please this tyrant.

Despite the reality that infants are totally physically dependent on adults, who's really in charge psychologically? The baby, of course! The baby is the center of his or her known universe and has dominion over all. This reality points toward the two basic psychological challenges of infancy.

Since infants have no capacity or concept of language, their reality and experience is feeling and emotionally based, an entity that I refer to as "emotional memory." At this stage of development a sound emotional perception or a dysfunctional one has significant permanent impact on the rest of a person's life.

The first and simultaneous developmental milestones are the establishment of "me versus not me" and "basic trust versus basic mistrust," phenomenological terminology developed by Dr. Eric Erikson. "Me versus not me" in psychological terminology is the development of "Ego," a Freudian term that is generally well-known and accepted. Ego is the function of the human mind when individuals are able to establish a sense of themselves as separate and discreet, but interactive with others in the real world. So, through consistent and constant parenting, the baby starts to recognize and interact with (smile) at repetitive family faces that usually smile in return.

This phenomenon is supported by brain research that has established a specific functional area of the visual brain (Area 4, fusiform face area) whose specific and sole function is to recognize and catalog faces. That's why babies almost always look you right in the face, eye to eye. This is evidence of the early phases of the lifelong process of cataloging faces and attaching emotional tags to each stored and cataloged face. I believe that this cognitive function is overlooked or undervalued in terms of its impact on our total emotional functioning. The baby, over time, comes to realize through this process that a mommy and daddy face exist, and they are not me. Wow! There is someone other than me in this existence! This development of ego is paramount to a person's ultimate capacity to deal with life; therefore, the developmental need is for consistent and continuous infant and parent—or stable parent surrogate, often grandma—interaction during the first twelve months of life is of such great importance.

Failures with this process can lead to "lacunae" or holes in ego function that can result in deficits in the ability to total inability to understand or deal with reality in later years, leading to some dysfunction or, in the extreme, to the total breakdown in function and/or reality perception, the psychiatric condition referred to as "psychosis."

This process and concept explains why those of us who are reasonably "sane" have such a struggle with people who are so obviously "insane." The life of the poor, disadvantaged human beings that populate the psychiatric wards of state institutions and the psychiatric units of hospitals and who chronically attend community mental health center clinics often believe that they are really God, Jesus, Muhammad, JFK, or the Virgin Mary while the true reality of their lives is tragically quite the opposite and totally dysfunctional. Why do they hear voices and develop a belief system that they are being watched and persecuted? Remember the crazy baby? The baby's perception is that it is all-powerful and the center of the universe. Babies can't speak nor do they have to in order to get their way. Babies have no idea or concept of God or Allah. When they grow up and develop language and the ability to conceptualize, they learn who God or Allah is and can attach a label or literal explanation to that crazy-baby experience that was originally stored in their emotional memory. It is from that point forward that they start to believe they are God or Allah despite the tragic realities of their lives.

I will never forget a nationally famous, and for the most part, high-functioning patient with Bipolar I Disorder whom I worked with years ago. This gentleman was educated, skilled, and had a top-level national security clearance. During one of our evening therapy sessions he leaned forward in his chair and with a manic, anxiety-producing, and bone-chilling smile confided the following to me: "You know, Doc, no matter what anyone says, you and I both know that I am Jesus Christ." How could this be? How could an educated and successful man believe that he was Jesus Christ? The answer relates back to his first developmental stage of life.

In psychiatry the technically applicable term here is "regression," the most serious psychological decompensation or level of dysfunction. Psychosis is a regression back to the emotional state and mental function of infancy. This is a state of mind where the boundaries of "me versus not me" are blurred or broken down completely. For example, people experiencing a severe ego dysfunction hear voices, experience auditory hallucinations. This is not the result of superior hearing acuity, although people suffering a psychotic episode can be and most often are hyper-vigilant. It is because the "me versus not me" function has broken down, and the individual cannot discriminate his or her internal thoughts or discussions from actual external auditory stimuli. Therefore, the vernacular term "nervous breakdown" is literally the breakdown in the psychological boundary between self and the not-self. Therefore, we have established a simplified understanding of ego and ego functioning and the resultant grandiose self-perception and auditory hallucinations when a person in effect defaults or "regresses" psychologically back to his or her infantile perception of the world.

The second psychological task of the first year explains why most people who experience psychotic regressions, ego dysfunctions, or nervous breakdowns often have feelings of being persecuted and may become clearly and frankly "paranoid." This mistrust of people and relationships is related to the successful or unsuccessful completion of the second and simultaneous task of early life.

Clearly, not only does the infant recognize there are other people populating his or her universe, possibly even more significantly, this is the infant's first experience at human relatedness. Once again, the old adage "You never get a second chance to make a first impression" truly applies here. This first experience is the cornerstone of the child's, and later the adult's, internalized or "gut" feeling about people and human relationships. Once again, the infant has no words to explain this experience, no literal memory, but it is nonetheless extremely important. It is the foundation, good or bad for the rest of life. Is this first human interaction loving, positive, supportive, protective, and relaxed or somewhere else on the opposite end of the spectrum where hatred, negativity, neglectfulness, hurt, and anxiety reside? In the first instance, the child's experience and later expectations of human relatedness stored in emotional memory are very positive. A basic trust in the goodness of human beings becomes intuitively woven into the fabric of the developing child's personality. The child eagerly reaches out to and engages others, at his or her emotional core believing that others care and want to be helpful and involved.

At the negative extreme, the imprinted initial or primary experience is hurtful. The resultant basic instinct of human relatedness that is imprinted for life is that you can't depend on others, physically or emotionally, and this leads to social isolation and an intense fear of engagement. At the negative extreme this can become frank paranoia, the belief that not only are others not going to be helpful, but they are actually out to get you or are planning to hurt you. Just like in the "me versus not me" experience, the child in this instance has no concept of time and language nor the ability to actually have a memory of these events the way adults have memory. This feeling or perception nonetheless is deeply woven into the fabric of personality and cannot be recalled as a specific chronologic event as such.

Unfortunately, in each individual's journey through life, this critical relatedness orientation tends to become a self-fulfilling prophecy. People with a positive perspective continuously seek and as a result tend to find the goodness in people and life's events, layering down real memories as proof of this pre-logical, pre-literal perception of relatedness. Human beings left with a negative perception layer down memories of experiences that validate their negative relatedness orientation. As I have pointed out to my past students, reality is just reality, but everyone's perception and interpretation of it is different and unique.

I like the analogy of a glass of water. Some will immediately respond to the stimulus that it's half empty while others will just as assuredly see it as half full. Another way of understanding this concept is as follows. As I am writing this morning, it's a warm sunny June day with a predicted high temperature of 82 degrees with low humidity and zero percent chance of rain. My feeling is, what a beautiful experience; my garden which includes many fragrant herbs and other decorative plants will grow robustly, energized by the spring sunshine; my world is good. A neighbor, on the other hand, sees it as another dry day: It won't be long before we are in a serious drought. Do I know how many new cases of skin cancer are going to be created by that malignant June sunlight? I love that bumper sticker from years ago—"Shit Happens." Thank you, mom and dad, for that positive first year because I still keep thinking that with persistent effort someday I am going to find the pony!

This foundational personality experience also generally explains some of the personality differences between siblings. Why are most first-born children more anxious, cautious, and security minded? My wife and I have two wonderful daughters and two equally wonderful granddaughters. All of us who have had children have figured out that when you have your first baby, it doesn't pop out with an instruction manual or instructional DVD attached! Who reads manuals or watches instructional DVDs anyway? After nine or so months there it is, a baby! It seems so helpless, small, and fragile. What if I mess up as a parent? you worry. You handle the infant with more care and anxiety then when helping dust and clean one of your grandmother's porcelain figurines. You seek and receive solicited and unsolicited advice from everyone, particularly from your mother and mother-in-law. They get overly involved in telling you what to do and absolutely what not to do. Sometimes I suspect their real motives are driven by guilt, trying not to allow you to mess up their darling grandchildren like they messed you up!

In any case, along came our first child, Susan. You have to keep in mind that Susan's father is a psychiatrist and her mother has a degree in elementary education and later becomes a licensed clinical social worker and psychotherapist. Despite all this education and experience, we're nervous first-time parents. Remember Susan didn't come with a manual or virtual reality training module! Baby Susan going through her first experience of human relatedness experiences her mother and father, despite their levels of education and experience, as not too competent and actually quite anxious. This experienced anxiety is woven into the core of her psychological fabric. This first very early childhood experience is almost always universal to first-time parents and their infants. It results in children who tend to be more cautious, worrisome, security- and goal-oriented, which are not necessarily bad things. Whenever I have asked for a show of hands during my lectures on child and adolescent development at the Eastern Virginia Medical School, the vast majority of medical students (80 percent or more) acknowledge that they are first-born children. Today, Susan is a practicing child psychologist and private school psychologist/administrator on the North Shore of the Boston, Massachusetts area. After all these years it never ceases to amaze me how predictable human behavior remains, but we will talk more about that later.

Continuing my narrative, four years later along came Samantha, or "Sam" as she is later known. This thought triggered what I believe was one smart thing my wife and I did as parents, which was in naming our daughters. We had no way of knowing what they would be like when they grew up. So, we gave them names with options to grow into. Our older daughter was named Susan Tracy so she could be Susan, Suzy, Sue, Tracy, etc. She turned out to be "Sue." Her sister was given Samantha Kimberly, so she could use Samantha, Sammy, Sam, Kimberly, Kim, etc. As previously mentioned, she became known as "Sam."

By the time of Sam's arrival, my wife and I were confident, relaxed old pros and basically didn't request or listen to any advice from our mothers, being pretty sure now that most of our enduring emotional hang-ups were likely their fault! It could be that the psychoanalysts got it right when their most famous patient, Woody Allen, nervously stated, "It all started with my mother." Anyway, all kidding aside, we didn't handle Sam like a porcelain figurine, as we were now experienced and learned about parenting, feeling quite competent. This feeling or emotional memory was ingrained into Sam at her psychological core and she basically grew up believing in people and life's goodness and opportunities.

This life-relatedness orientation played out in our daughters' personalities when they were both about four years of age. Susan encountered a strange dog at the park that was sitting on a woman's lap. The dog was small, quite furry, and seemed friendly enough. Susan approached slowly, tentatively and cautiously stretching out her right hand, arm fully extended should a quick withdrawal be warranted. She was clearly fascinated with and would have loved to touch or pet the "nice doggy." Unfortunately, and quite understandably since the dog sensed my daughter's anxiety, it stood up on its owner's lap and let out a sharp bark. Susan reflexively and quickly withdrew her hand. The encounter with the "nice doggy" was over. Susan retreated to the security of her mother's side. This small emotional "owie," as my now child psychologist daughter Sue refers to such experiences, further reinforced her cautious orientation to the world at large.

Sam, at about the same age, encountered a very large dog walking beside its owner, controlled by a short, stout leather tether. She directly approached this very large "nice bow-wow" without hesitation and started petting and scratching its head and neck. The dog accepted this interaction with tolerance or even some level of enjoyment as evidenced by its licking her face and wagging its tail, before mommy pulled her back explaining that one should never approach an unfamiliar dog with such devil-may-care behavior. However, Sam had already experienced another event that confirmed her generally positive perception of "her" world. I believe that this positive orientation to life and the willingness to take a risk led Sam to her marriage to J. L., an accomplished screenwriter and director of note (Bobby G. Can't Swim and Off Jackson Avenue)—not that it was risky to marry J. L., but she is totally simpatico with his artistry, creativity, and outside-the-box thinking. Both are members of the Screen Actors Guild. Sam, in her own right, is respected and recognized in the international art world. She definitely became the greater risk taker of my two daughters, typical of a second child.

The road of life reaches out for years and years into the distance, far beyond our ability to see or predict. It hopefully will have many smooth stretches with beautiful scenery, but inevitably it will also have many potholes and hazards. The potholes and their negative impact seem to stay with us more than the miles and miles of smooth travel. This unfortunately seems to be the true psychological nature of human beings, to focus on the negative, psychologically tabbing and holding onto the negative events of our life's experience, over and over again.

This completes a rather synoptic version of the first psychological year of life. It's important to remember that all of this occurs prior to the development of language, that this phase is more experiential, emotional, without logic, non-temporal, non-historical, nor factual. Yet, the emotional memory established has a lasting, personality-shaping impact on all of us and our individual perceptions of reality, human relatedness, and our overall ability to function.

Based on all the forgoing, I would like to pose some concepts for my non-therapist readers. The first thought is that you cannot change genetics, unless of course this book is read in the twenty-second century and medical science has mastered genetic engineering. You have to honestly look at your parents and first relatives. In my initial evaluation of people, I always ask if there is any family history of emotional disorders or chemical dependency problems. You need to ask yourself these questions, and be honest. If you don't know the answer or answers, ask your parents, who probably won't answer accurately or honestly anyway, or if possible, a close relative who just might be less biased. If there is a verifiable history of emotional or chemical dependency problems, then you should do some homework. Go to the library or use the Internet. Go to sites that are reputable like WebMD. com, keeping in mind that the old saying "Paper never refused ink" applies even more so to the Web, that it can be as much a source of misinformation or disinformation as information.

Evaluate yourself! You really can. Let me help you. In research and survey methodology, a "0" to "10" scale system is often effectively used. In this type of evaluative system using mood or feeling as the focus, rate yourself as honestly and as accurately as possible. I explain during my initial evaluation, "0" is being totally miserable and hopeless, with the only reasonable alternative being to commit suicide; "10" is the happiest person you could ever imagine being; "5" is the average person for your age group, gender, etc. If you rate yourself as anything other than a "5," identify two or three reasons why this is so. For anxiety, "0" is totally calm and relaxed and "10" is freaking out, going insane with worry. Once again, try to identify two or three reasons you are on either side of "5." Apply the scale to those areas of your life that you see as most important, having the most emotional impact, positive or negative. Apply what you have learned in this chapter and the chapters that follow. If your scale scores do not improve at least to some degree, consider getting professional help. I should point out that these early months of life in psychiatric parlance are referred to as the "oral phase" of psychological development. Logically, it is identified as such because baby puts everything in its mouth. But, more importantly, orality is essential in a primary way to the establishment of human relatedness, physical nutrition, and emotional gratification. Breast-feeding or taking the bottle while being held at this stage of development is essentially the singular source of meaningful, sensual, fulfilling experience for the infant; therefore, it is a powerful, primary emotional memory influence.

Taking a break, but a related aside from this narrative, this stage of development may psychologically explain humanity's valuation of a woman's breasts. Why is there such an apparent societal fixation? Why are plastic surgeons making hundreds of millions of dollars annually performing breast augmentations? Why are more millions spent on devices, pills, creams, or lotions that guarantee an increase in cup size? Why size-enhancing bras? How do we explain the American Medical Association estimate for 2005 that 335,000 women eighteen years of age and younger had breast augmentations? That number was projected to increase to more than half a million annually by 2007. As you will see later, some of this phenomenon is just basic marketing, but there is a more basic psychologically, pre-cognitive, pre-logical etiology that can also explain this phenomenon.

Think about the crazy baby. The infant's first experience of nourishment, oral gratification, and a sense of warmth and loving relatedness takes place during breast-feeding. Anatomically and physiologically during pregnancy, the mother's breasts enlarge greatly so that she can provide adequate lactation (milk), so the baby can be nourished. When the infant is ready to engage in nursing, consider the real-time physical perspective. The baby's head is relatively small and the mother's breast by comparison is large, quite often actually being bigger than the baby's head. Although the infant has no real memory of the event, he or she has emotional memory that is deeply established at their psyche's core. The baby's perspective of this memory is that whatever this intensely emotionally fulfilling and physically nourishing thing is, it's "humongous"! That is why women react to another woman's breasts equally as much as their male counterparts. What about those babies that are bottle-fed you ask? In that situation the baby is still held against the woman's warm, enlarged mammary while sucking at the bottle. Consider also the size of the nipple equivalent part of the baby's bottle. It's huge! Psychologically, this means that the fascination with this part of the female anatomy really isn't an obsession, compulsion, perversion, or sexual-orientation issue but a normal developmental part of emotional memory, both sexes being affected equally. The psychological terminology applicable here is "cathected," meaning that there is a strong positive or negative emotional charge, tag, feeling, or value, usually sexual in nature, attached to and elicited by a specific object, in this specific case the breasts of women.

Back on track now, if you have evidence historically that your emotional struggles may be genetically based upon family history, then you may have to accept the possibility that medication will be a major and integral part of your overall treatment. If you are already in therapy or counseling, be aware of your "gut feeling" about your therapist, as this feeling may be your emotional memory at work in real time. Remember that part of the human brain functions to recognize face versus object. Therefore, each of us has a catalog of faces to which we have attached emotional memory tags. This emotional attachment or tag may be positive or negative, but it is established to a great extent during your pre-logical, pre-literal oral developmental phase.

You surely have experienced a reaction upon first meeting a new person that doesn't make any sense whatsoever. This gut feeling will probably be labeled by your therapist as "transference," or a transfer of feeling out of your emotional memory bank, attached now to the person in front of you, whether that happens to be your therapist or a random person who revolves through your life. People often transfer or attribute so many qualities to their therapist that have no basis in fact or reality. This process occurs to a greater or lesser degree with everyone you meet or interact with. It's your therapist's job to access and clarify this mental catalog of faces and the attached emotional memory, often "analyzing" the transference. Through this kind of therapeutic work you can gain better insight into why you feel and act or react the way you do, and then you can possibly change undesirable, self-defeating behavior patterns into more fulfilling and self-enhancing behavior patterns and life experiences.

Now to my therapist colleagues, let me share some thoughts on how emotional insult or trauma, either by action or inaction, can affect your working with people. As I pointed out earlier, you can't change genetics. I mentioned that many psychiatric illnesses or syndromes are at least in part, if not in large part, "neuropsychophysiologic" in nature to a great extent, are secondary to genetic coding; therefore, so-called "talking therapy" or trying to talk a paranoid patient out of delusional thoughts or telling a manic patient, "don't

be so emotional," or demanding that an ADD patient "pay attention" is really an exercise in futility and of little therapeutic value—it
may even be counterproductive or emotionally damaging.

This reality slapped me right in the face during my residency
at the Institute of Pennsylvania Hospital, historically the first psychiatric hospital in America. During my final year of training I was
called to see and work up a new patient, who as it turns out was
a well-known professor at one of the many Philadelphia medical
schools. During my interview with this physician, I noticed that he
spoke at a whisper level and gazed continuously and hypervigilant-
ly, repeatedly scanning the room. When I queried as to why he was
behaving in such a manner, he warned me that "they" were watching him through a hidden camera behind the decorative mirror in
his room and that "they" were recording our every word through a
"bug" in the chandelier-like light fixture. Despite my efforts to dis-
suade him of this obvious paranoid delusion, he persisted. Finally,
clearly demonstrating my inexperience as a young psychiatrist, I na-
ively decided to show the doctor that what he believed was, in fact,
not true. Since the historic, elegant, old Institute had high ceilings,
rendering the chandelier fixture well out of my reach, and knowing I couldn't fly, proving that my reality testing was intact, at least
compared to the physician/patient, I stood up and went directly to
the mirror in question and moved it aside to show the deranged
professor that there was, indeed, no camera behind the mirror.

Feeling a moment of therapeutic triumph I stated, "See, doctor,
there is no camera." But rather than acknowledging the truth of my
less-than-brilliant intervention, he seemed saddened and discour-
aged. I have never forgotten his deflating words: "See how good
they are. They knew you were going to do that, and they moved it
to another spot before you got there." So much for talking therapy!
A series of six electroconvulsive treatments (ECTs) and the professor had a complete recovery, eventually returning to achieve many
years of distinguished academic work. The moral of the story is that
with a psychotic regression, the person in such a state of mind has
gone back to a pre-language, pre-literal functional level, rendering
"talking therapy" essentially meaningless and useless.

Similarly, I caution the enthusiasm of those people working with
early traumatized, neglected children. They are the most needy and

yet the least accessible to therapeutic intervention or human relatedness. Their ego structure, the "me versus not me" function, is so impaired that they easily can regress back into a psychotic or psychotic-like state of mind with the smallest amount of stress or disappointment. The faces in their mental catalog are almost all tagged with negative, horrific emotional memories. The care and treatment of these patients plagued with negative emotional memory are, to say the least, daunting.

I have some words of advice for those who are undaunted by the insurmountable task of treating these emotionally damaged children. The process of healing takes a very, very long time—measured in years, not weeks or months—so you must first of all be extremely patient. You must realize that it is not just your words—the ego injuries occurred for the most part long prior to the development of language—therefore, these children are little impacted by words. Greater therapeutic gain comes from consistency and general demeanor. I have counseled my inpatient and residential program therapists to make every attempt to see their patients about the same time each day. Although emotional memory is layered down when there is no real sense or concept of time, there is a diurnal rhythm of light and darkness, a pattern to the taking of meals. This principle of therapeutic and environmental consistency can also be applied to outpatient therapy.

More than thirty years ago, after I completed an active-duty stint with the U.S. Navy, I was referred a young man who had sustained a "nervous breakdown" while serving on active duty during the Vietnam conflict. He had spent months as an inpatient on the neuropsychiatric ward of the Portsmouth Naval Hospital. He was discharged from active duty with a disability rating and referred to the Veterans Administration hospital, where he spent months and months on the various inpatient wards. His response to his treatment plan and overall functioning did not go well. He ended up spending more than 150 days in inpatient psychiatric units, and when not hospitalized he stayed holed up in his parents' home, unkempt, unshaved, un-bathed, and sleeping ten to fourteen hours a day. When not asleep he paced constantly and seemed frightened or suspicious of everyone, including his own mother and father, brother and sisters. Eventually, a social worker at the VA hospital proposed that something different be tried as his inpatient stays and emergency room visits as well as scheduled and unscheduled visits to outpatient departments were not decreasing in frequency nor was the intensity of his mental illness and its negative impact on the veteran and his family. The social worker had heard through the grapevine that I had worked with some of the heroic naval aviators who had served long stretches of time at the "Hanoi Hilton" as POWs. The veteran was issued a "special" card that allowed him to see me on a weekly basis, more frequently if necessary, and so started my journey down the highway of life with Bill (a fictitious name).

First of all, Bill had a severe genetically based psychiatric illness that predated his "nervous breakdown," as he was want to call it. Accordingly, a core part of his treatment plan was medication to address the neurophysiologic dysfunction in his brain circuitry. Over the years his medications had included first- and second-generation antipsychotics. They were clearly helpful but had not been enough to curtail his previous need for inpatient and emergency services. As I listened to Bill in the early going, he told me that he liked his first Navy psychiatrist, who happened to have been of Hispanic origin, and felt the psychiatrist had helped him the most. However, once he was discharged from the Naval hospital inpatient unit and was transferred to the barracks on the hospital grounds, he was assigned a new psychiatrist, which was very disappointing and disorienting, leading to a readmission to the inpatient unit and a reunion with the Hispanic physician. This time around, once he was re-stabilized, he was discharged home and his care fell to the regional VA hospital. His course at the VA hospital, as noted earlier, was very unstable, his behavior extremely dysfunctional. Hence the special card was issued. Now the referring social worker told Bill and his family that I was this "hot shot" young psychiatrist who could really help him. Although we all love flattery, it was probably closer to the truth that the VA was grasping at straws to bring about some change, any change, and to get Bill out of their hair or "dump" him, at least temporarily, so they hoped. At least the VA staff established an initial potentially positive transference by emphasizing that I was the one psychiatrist who could help—and, as it turned out, my foreign face didn't hurt either.

Bill and I started down that highway of life that for many miles and years had a smooth surface and beautiful scenery along the way, but it also had many potholes and hazards, like the death of his father and eventually his mother. He was never able to significantly overcome the faces tagged with negative emotional memory that his mind had cataloged. All people were viewed without logic or reason as untrustworthy, sinister, and potentially dangerous, a perception that was also held and reconfirmed every day by his mother while she was alive. I believe that mother and son actually shared the same mental illness from a genetic standpoint. Luckily for me, somewhere in his pre-logical emotional memory he had no tagged gut feeling or emotional memory to a psychiatrist with a foreign-looking face, Hispanic or Asian. Therefore, we were off to a good start. But most important was what I learned early on by listening.

It became clear that consistency and stability and the familiarity of my face, if you will, were critical. Bill needed to catalog or re-catalog and somehow change his emotional memory tags to some faces, specifically my face! This was established in various ways. First of all, I essentially saw Bill every Monday at the same time (1 p.m.) for more than thirty years until he passed away. I tried my best to be punctual, being a little late on fewer than twenty occasions in more than 1,500 therapy sessions. Bill eventually shared with me that he could not explain why, but no matter how bad his life was going or how distraught and upset he felt, he could "hang in there" because Monday at 1 p.m. was always there for him.

Now, there were times I was away from the practice for family events or holiday, but I always prepared Bill for my absences long in advance and pointed out that he could talk to or see, on an emergency basis, any one of the physicians in my office while I was away. He never actually exercised this particular option but always demonstrated some level of regression or decompensation if Monday at 1 p.m. didn't happen. Remember, Bill and almost all the people under our care and guidance have emotional memory tags that are preconscious and non-logical "gut feelings," always seeing the glass as half empty or worse. They believe that "shit happens" and there definitely is no pony! They anticipate that the faces encountered in their lives are insincere at best or sinister at worst. If you cancel regularly or show up late with any frequency, this process just reconfirms and reinforces their core negative perception of human caring and relatedness. This effect, although probably not expressed, will interfere with any positive therapeutic work that might be accomplished. Even if the therapist sincerely apologizes for frequent tardiness, eventually this pattern will cause a patient to think or more importantly "feel" that the therapist does not really care about me or cannot manage his or her own life, so how can he or she help me manage mine?

So what about Bill? In the thirty years under my care he never spent another day in a psychiatric hospital inpatient unit. He did do some volunteer work now and again for his church, which he found to be somewhat fulfilling. He dated a woman for a while, but never married. He did have a border collie which he named "Buddy," the name that his father used to call him when he was a child. He enjoyed Buddy, "because he loves me and always wants to be with me." Bill had a relatively good and stable life until his passing from heart disease.

Ten years into the treatment with me, Bill got a notice that his disability status needed to be reviewed and reevaluated by the Veterans Administration. He was very anxious about this situation, worrying that he would lose his monthly VA disability check or lose me as his psychiatrist. I reassured him that everything would work out fine, but Bill was a glass-half-empty person and suffered greatly, demonstrating some regressed behaviors right up until the fateful day when he had to travel to a different VA hospital for his ten-year evaluation.

Bill got permanent life disability and unlimited certification to see me! What was the key question that clinched the deal? The VA psychiatrist asked Bill how many days he had spent in an inpatient facility since he started working with me. When he responded "none," the woman physician seemed incredulous at first and asked whether Bill understood the question. When she realized that he did comprehend, and that the answer was still "none," Bill reported that she told him he should continue to see me and openly wondered what I was doing to keep him so stable functionally. The answer was not just adequate medication management and every Monday at 1 p.m., but also directing Bill to think about some of the smooth stretches of life's highway and the beautiful scenery.

You see, Bill loved the Atlanta Braves, the Carolina Tarheels,

Buddy, and his Harley-Davidson. Although we clearly discussed, looked at, and worked on decreasing the psychological fallout from his areas of emotional conflict and pain, I always intentionally directed a portion of each therapy session to one of his positive things, memories thereof, and plans for the future. I could never move Bill to be anywhere near even a glass-half-full guy, but I was able to move him away from his near total paranoia and emotional isolation to being trusting enough to reach out somewhat as evidenced by his eventual involvement in some of his church's charitable community activities. He even traveled to Atlanta and Chapel Hill on one or two occasions to attend games played by his Braves and Tarheels. The Braves and the Tarheels represented traditions of winning, and Bill's identification with winning was emotionally important for him. Buddy was obviously unconditional love. The Harley represented his longing for rebellion and freedom—sadly, states he never did achieve to any significant degree.

So, to my young future therapists as well as seasoned colleagues, in our own humanity we may have a tendency, like the people we work with, to focus on what's wrong. It is human nature to dwell on the negative, as evidenced by the general public's fascination with the tabloids and talk-show hosts like Maury, Montel, and Jerry. And while it may be our job to look at negative events and experiences and behavior patterns, I suggest focusing at least a small portion of each therapy session on looking back at some of the smooth stretches of life's highway and what has been right! If we focus only on the potholes, we may be directly or subliminally reinforcing the negative emotional constructs of the people we so much want to help to change.

This same principle applies to all of us, even if we should never need help or seek counseling. I would suggest that at least once a week, twice if possible, take fifteen to twenty minutes and find your private quiet space. Mine is the back deck of our condo surrounded by my herb garden, flowering vines, bushes, and trees. Sit quietly and clear your mind of your current life's struggles and any conflicted emotions that challenge you, and recall from memory, especially with the emotional content being included, some of the stretches of your personal life's highway when the road was really smooth, the sun was shining warmly, the scenery was beautiful, and your life was good. Although it will take some time and commitment on your part to do this, you will be able to alter some aspects of your own emotional memory in a positive, self-therapeutic way. This particular Tsaoism may be obvious and suggested in various forms by many before me, but the following one may be less so.

I mentioned that I was honored to work with POWs, American heroes who suffered the premeditated torture of the "Hanoi Hilton." They suffered physical pain, starvation, and brainwashing. Talk about making lemonade out of lemons! Despite all this they never lost a love of county, family, and God! The two POWs that I was privileged to spend the most time with both said they would do it again. What an amazing example of courage and commitment! Despite this strength of character they both were eventually broken and signed confessions stating that they were guilty of committing war crimes. How could this possibly be? How could this have happened?

I would like to point out here that the basic principle and foundation of brainwashing and modern-day marketing is "thought insertion." The human mind is incapable of resisting a thought insertion! I would challenge you, as I have done so often to my medical students, interns, and resident psychiatrists, with all the psychological resistance you can muster to try not to think about a polar bear. As soon as you've read this, you see the furry white fellow lumbering along the Arctic Ice.

Accepting that thought insertion is an irresistible mind game tactic that has been used most effectively for evil, here comes the lemonade. Brainwash yourself in a positive, constructive way. It is our nature to remember the potholes and accidents along the road of life. In effect, we constantly experience negative thought insertions continuously generated by our own minds or inserted by others, like the news media. Therefore, use a positive thought insertion to break the negative Cassandra cycle. Where taking fifteen to twenty minutes a week, as was previously recommended, is a proactive suggested action, positive or proactive thought insertion is a reactive suggestion that you can utilize, anytime, anywhere. My personal tactic, when in a negative cognitive cycle or funk, is to insert my granddaughters via a picture of them I carry with me everywhere I go. Within seconds my psychic world is a much better place! I've actually progressed using this personal intervention to the point that I no longer need the actual picture any longer in order to right my emotional ship. Find your own positive thought insertion method or technique. Brainwash yourself whenever necessary. If you do this, as the Oracle in the Matrix movie said, "You'll feel just fine." Trust me. It works! You might even be able to avoid the need of ever having to visit a mental health professional, which alone is worth the time, effort, and money you have invested in this book.

One last sobering thought to my brethren in the mental health field: There is a tragically sad truth that I learned many years ago when I was the medical director of a residential facility near Williamsburg, Virginia. Part of my duties was to train the mental health techs and young future program therapists. I was impressed with their idealism and almost unlimited enthusiasm to help the poor emotionally damaged children and adolescent residents at the facility. I pointed out that despite their, at times, heroic efforts to "make a difference" in these children's lives, they, like all those who have gone before them, will eventually "abandon" each and every child as a result of moving on in pursuit of their own professional careers or the child moving on as a result of discharge or transfer. Despite the story of Bill and me, few realistic opportunities will ever exist for you to travel to the end of life's highway with any given client or patient. But this book may help you alter, to some degree, their pre-language emotional memory orientation, or help them through a developmental stage with its many challenges and potholes.

To all my readers, you cannot underestimate the importance and impact of parenting, good or bad, on your child's eventual orientation to life and his or her ultimate emotional strength and stability. As you read this, your genetics, layered-down emotional memory, and emotionally tagged faces are all but chiseled in stone. But this reality doesn't mean that by following some of the suggestions in this book you can't gradually chip away at the stone and bring about real change. At the very least, armed with this knowledge you can make a difference for your children, grandchildren, and, if blessed, great-grandchildren.

2

Smiling Elmo

Now we move on to the next stage of emotional development. Assuming that the earlier oral phase was completed reasonably well from a psychological developmental standpoint, and always keeping in mind the power of genetics, the infant transitions to the "anal phase." This developmental time is identified as the anal phase because at this juncture in time the parents or parent surrogates generally become obsessed with toilet training and its need for completion. Whereas problems in the oral phase can developmentally lead to or predispose a person to the most serious of psychological breakdowns or regressions—psychosis; dysfunction in this second phase of development leads to or predisposes toward varying degrees of personality traits or to the more severely debilitating personality disorders.

This time in the child's life is often referred to as the "terrible twos." Why so "terrible"? From the parents' perspective it is initially a time of great triumph: baby's first steps! Then the "terrible" reality, the baby is mobile! Dangers lurk everywhere, around every corner. Stairs to trip up or fall down, dangerous sharp corners or edges right at head level, the family dog or cat, poisonous chemicals in the cabinet below the kitchen sink, and countless other dangers. When the baby gets up, this monarch of the universe, the epicenter of everything, the omnipotent and all-powerful, the ruler of all there is, for the first time in his or her life hears the prohibition "No! No!" These negative words are associated with the disapproving mommy or daddy face. Wow! There are limits. I can't believe that I can't do what I want to do when I want to do it! The "not me's" won't let me do certain things and encourage me to do others. This is nowhere near as much fun as being emperor of the universe, and the baby cries, screams, throws a temper tantrum, refuses to move when asked to do so, and takes on a strong resemblance to a heavy sack of potatoes when finally picked up and physically moved by mommy or daddy.

What a letdown it must be going from the lofty heights of absolute sovereign of all to having to acquiesce, albeit grudgingly, at times to the not me mommy and daddy face. Thus the battle lines are drawn. The battle rages between pure, narcissistic immediate gratification, the "Id" in Freudian terms, and the drive to please the mommy face and daddy face, and finally the acceptance that the not me's can indeed control me physically, if necessary. However, Gandhi's life demonstrated that you can be shackled physically but never give up the battle mentally or emotionally. One might say that Gandhi employed the tactics of a two-year-old when he laid down across the railroad tracks in India in protest and refused to move. He proclaimed that, in fact, he was doing nothing at all but lying there "passive" while totally bringing all train traffic to a complete halt "aggressive."

So it is that we will resort to manipulation and deception when faced with overwhelming physical force. Gandhi won world acclaim for such behavior and the ultimate success of his cause, while children are quite differently viewed as stubborn, bad, or both, seen as being infuriatingly "passive-aggressive."

This struggle between parent and child and its resolution are of major psychological significance. Proper parent-child interaction helps to establish a basic concept of right and wrong. This right versus wrong value system is referred to as "Superego," from the Latin supra, meaning "above," and "ego," the cognitive function that mediates our perception of reality. In other words, it is the primitive or the early beginnings of a basic conceptualization of right versus wrong "superimposed" on one's concept of reality.

Since right versus wrong seems to be such a legal thing, I often tease my friends who practice in the field of law that if superego is a value system superimposed on your sense of reality, then what is the literal interpretation of the legal term subpoena? I suppose it also must be from the Latin sub, or "below." So when you are served with that piece of paper, they've got you below the "poena," or by the proverbial you know what's! Just joking of course. Really!

It really doesn't take a psychiatrist, psychologist, or other mental health professional to see the importance of developing a superego or "conscience" in addition to having a solid foundation to see and deal with reality. It all starts with a simple "No! No!" and grows in scope and complexity over the years, from a simple "don't hit the dog" through "why it's wrong to litter," eventually to the morality of the death penalty. So, superego starts humbly with the interaction of a parent and child and reaches a zenith in the deliberations and opinions of the Supreme Court of the United States. Thus the conscious and psychological task of the anal phase of development is to understand and accept a value system fostered by the parental faces and other faces of emotional importance such as grandparents, nannies, daycare providers, and relatives. As in the initial phase of emotional development, there is also layered down in memory during this phase of development an emotional tag to another cataloged face, the baby's own face! And like the impact of the oral phase, this emotional tag tends to be lifelong and is ever present just under the surface, quickly able to burst on top at a moment's notice following any stimulus, external or internal, that causes us to look at our own face in the psychological mirror, whether emotional memory tagged with an extreme positive or extreme negative or somewhere in between.

"No! No!" starts limit setting in our lives; as one of my granddaughters has said with considerable conviction on occasion, "I don't like it!" Nor do other children like it. "No!" is the beginning of a comprehension of what we are not supposed to do, but it is toilet or potty training that gives the baby a sense of what to do or what not to do with "doo-doo." Parents are really into potty training for a number of reasons. First of all, they are by now sick of changing diapers, using wipes to clean poopy off the baby's bottom, and carrying all of the necessary paraphernalia whenever you take baby anywhere away from home base. Parents also may be buckling to some degree of peer pressure, hearing that their good friends' baby was fully trained at a much younger age, or spurred on by the baby's grandmother recalling that mom or dad was fully trained much earlier, implying the not-too-subtle message that mom and dad are not doing an adequate job, probably far from it.

When should you start toilet training? What should be your attitude or appropriate approach to this important task of child rearing and emotional development?

Let's start with the neurologic or physical reality. It's all a matter of "nerves." Really it is! Most healthy babies come equipped with legs and feet. So why don't they walk independently right from the get-go? Some say that it's because the baby's feet are too small. Others say it's that the baby's head is much too big, resulting in the baby being too top-heavy—the opposite of Weebles that may wobble but never fall down—that the slightest misstep would lead to the immediate invocation of the laws of gravity and over the kid would topple, definitely landing on its head! But these hypotheses aren't logically, scientifically, or neurologically accurate. Once a child gets up and starts walking around, generally around twelve months of age, his feet are still comparatively too small and his head is still much too big. Therefore, this hypothesis cannot logically be the explanation.

The actual explanation is in "myelination." When a baby is born, it has a brain, spinal cord, and nerves, not dissimilar to a house while under construction that has been fully wired electrically. Picture in your mind that all of the major electrical wiring to the heating and air systems and the kitchen appliances are fully insulated but the rest of the wiring in the house is not. Would that be a mess or what?

Neurologically, the baby has all these "wires," or neurons, that stretch from the top of its head to the tips of its toes, but all are not totally insulated, myelinated. In medical terms the myelination process occurs rostra-caudal, meaning from nose to tail. So at birth and for months thereafter, the baby has no voluntary or effective control of those body functions to which the nerves have not been myelinated. This process progresses through the multiplication and growth of fatty cells, "the cells of Schwann," that eventually sheath and insulate all the nerves in the baby's nervous system.

In those early months as the baby's visual acuity improves, it can see its hands and feet but cannot purposefully move them. They move at this stage of development as a result of reflex action. So, early on, if you put your finger in the baby's palm, it will reflectively close its fingers. Often this is mistakenly seen by parents as a sign of recognition or affection. Not so! It takes many months for the rostra-caudal process to reach completion. Until the baby's neurons are all insulated, the un-insulated areas remain, in effect, shorted out, having only involuntary or reflex movement—demonstrated when the doctor hits you with the rubber hammer just below the kneecap and your leg jumps. Therefore, as this nose-to-tail process unfolds, more and more of the baby's neurologic systems come online; where grasping to touch stimulus was without conscious perception, it now becomes a purposeful conscious act by the baby often associated with eye contact as face cataloging and emotional tagging are an ongoing and continuous process. As the baby gains more and more conscious control, it gains the ability to purposely control its arms, shoulders, and upper torso to the point that it can roll over and pull itself up and stand upright while holding on for support and balance.

As myelination progresses lower or caudally, eventually the nerve tracks that control the lower extremities come online and the baby can start to walk. With this event the process of "No! No!" begins, through which the baby learns the right or acceptable things to do versus the wrong or unacceptable things not to do. Simultaneously, the baby is developing its own internalized emotional self-face through this process. This is the natural progression, following the first, primary, and ongoing experience of human relatedness. The attitude and actions of the mommy face and daddy face, now "mommy" and "daddy," mold the baby's perception of its own emotional face and associated tag. Looking in the psychological mirror, is it a good face or bad face? What is a parent to do? When a baby toddles toward the down staircase or wants to touch the glowing coils of the oven top do you let them? Of course not!! The baby has no concept of serious injury or life-threatening danger.

I once had an extremely uninvolved stepfather, an advocate of the "school of hard knocks" method of parenting, relating to the glowing stovetop coil example, say, "I bet the little shit won't touch it again if you let 'm."

Barring the learning by third-degree burn plan of inaction, how should parents react or behave? Obviously, no responsible parent would ever knowingly, through action or inaction, put his or her child in harm's way. What is important is the attitude of the parents and how he or she goes about it. As in the first developmental stage where there is little to no literal actual memory, most of what is saved at this stage is similarly emotional, non-logical, non-temporal, but imprinted in indelible ink deep in our minds nonetheless. Some of the behavioral and emotional responses to children may be out of the parent's own emotional control, the parental relatedness to the child being altered by the parent's own internalized faces and ingrained behavioral responses to human interaction. Part may actually be the babies themselves!

Published studies have shown that different infants, from birth, have a more or less relentless nature while others clearly don't. One research group measured how long infants would suck at a bottle while getting no milk for their effort. Some of the babies sucked at the non-giving bottle just a few times and then passively gave up, while others would persist almost indefinitely. Most parents would tell me they got the latter kid, stubbornly never giving up on getting into trouble or always wanting it his or her way!

Despite the effect of genetics, what is the emotional imprinting process that occurs simultaneously to the developing concept of right and wrong? Once the baby has to step down from his or her regal throne, what emotional tag will be attached to his or her own emotional face? Coincidental or not, this all happens around potty training time. The Bard of Avon once said that this all may be "much ado about nothing." Psychologically, it is a time to make much ado about doo-doo! So, let's take a closer look at the ground rules for toilet training.

The first question is should you spend your hard-earned $19.95 on the plastic potty with the smiling face of Elmo staring at your baby's derriere? Psychologically, the answer is emphatically yes! It is money well spent! Consider the fact that your baby is now taking great interest in toddling around and experiencing all that it possibly can. During the course of daily events the baby witnesses from the safety of your arms, or more frighteningly at eye level, up close and personal, that when the handle of the toilet is pressed down, anything, either floating or submerged, in this large porcelain enclosed body of water is sucked down and away by a powerful swirling vortex accompanied by the whooshing sound of rushing water, to disappear never to be seen again! That's right, never to be seen again! Gone forever! Having witnessed this event, do you think that the baby might have some worry or concern should you attempt to balance baby on the regular toilet seat or the toilet seat potty adapter? Believe me, the $19.95 is money well spent on the smiling Elmo potty. Would you want to be sucked into oblivion via a watery vortex to the frightening sound of rushing water? I think not. If you give it some thought, despite the advantage of not having to handle the baby's business any longer, consider that from the baby's perspective, smiling Elmo is much, much less anxiety producing. As mentioned earlier, we as parents have many practical, emotional, and competitive reasons to complete the toilet training of our children as soon as possible, if not even sooner. But, before we get into technique, let's spend a few minutes on proper timing. When should you start?

I have heard many theories and suggestions on this particular matter. Some suggest that you start as soon as possible, as early as six months when the baby can sit up. These very observant, and possibly obsessively driven, parents have observed the physiologic gastrointestinal response—that fairly shortly after you have put something into your baby's mouth, something comes out the other end! These parents feed their child, wait the previously observed and noted amount of time, and then sit the child down with Elmo or suspend the baby over the impending vortex. The evacuation event occurs on schedule, and they triumphantly report that their child was "potty trained" by nine months of age or even younger. To this bit of reported historical information, I often think to myself, The Yankees could probably use a consistent backup catcher, and Mom and Dad, you two seem to fit the bill nicely! The reason for this opinion is that at six months of age the infant has no voluntary control of its wee-wee or poo-poo and these parents have simply observed the usual gastrointestinal time sequence and have learned to "catch" whatever falls out of the other end!

There was a doll on the market years ago that simulated this phenomenon extremely well. The child would feed the doll its bottle, in this case filled with water. From the doll's mouth to its bottom was a plastic tube. So, shortly after the child gave the doll the bottle, as the world-famous chef often proclaims, "Bam! There it is," a wet diaper! "Yeah baby!"

At the other end of the spectrum people have told me that the right time to start toilet training is "when the child's ready." Does this mean that parents should patiently wait until age five or six when one day the child announces matter-of-factly at the breakfast table, "I'm ready now"? Come on now, this system doesn't make much sense either. A reasonable time to start toilet training must exist somewhere between these two extremes.

Remember myelination and its rostra-caudal progression? Recall that insulation of the human wiring progresses nose to tail. Tail? Hmm. We humans don't have tails! We only have the evolutionary ruminants of a tail seen in the bones at the end of our spine, the coccyx bone, the "tailbone." The nerves at the end of the tail become functional or are myelinated last in the sequence of the nose-to-tail event, and guess what those nerves affect related to voluntary control? You guessed it, the control of urination and defecation! So what is a good rule of thumb? Start toilet training about twelve to sixteen weeks after the baby can walk on its on, when the child has some voluntary control over its own wee-wee and poo-poo functions. If you start too early, you will unfairly pressure the child to do something it really cannot do, which may result in high levels of anxiety and a sense of failure that can eventually lead to personal low self-esteem or worse. To the other extreme, if you start too late, the child may never develop any sense of anxiety or a need to please others, another undesirable outcome.

Equally as important during this phase of early superego formation is the parent's attitude toward the whole process. Remember that the child is developing the emotional tag to their own internalized emotional face, which will affect them for the rest of their lives. Assuming that you have now spent the money on the smiling Elmo potty, Elmo's countenance is a helpful hint from the manufacturer about how you should go about the whole process. Using the catcher's mentality, but not starting too early based on scientific reality, we know that shortly after fluid or solid food intake the baby will normally proceed to eliminate #1 or #2. You quickly remove the hopefully still-clean diaper and sit the child down on the Elmo throne. Presenting the most positive mommy or daddy face, you offer encouragement. You say things like "Come on, honey, you can do it. Do it for mommy" or similar such words. You often resort to bribes like some sort of sweet treat or a variation of the magical element, chocolate, a most important member of one of the essential food groups, at least to those who love chocolate. And when baby delivers the "goods," so to speak, what a great event it is! You applaud, and grinning from ear to ear, praise the child for delivering this wonderful "gift" to mommy and daddy. And if you have been through this phase of your child's life before, you know what a "gift" it truly is. But consider this: Think about how silly you must really look.

Here you are, grown adults, clapping, rejoicing, raising a big fuss over this "gift," a pile of brown stuff that frankly smells like shit! That's because it is shit! But how you react is nonetheless fundamental to your child's self-esteem, self-image, and cataloged emotional self-face. So, keep on clapping and praising despite the obvious stench.

If you overdo it, two potential outcomes are possible. First, and probably the least problematic, is that because of "the great to-do about doo-doo" the child will believe the result of his or her bowel movement is really valuable and truly worth saving. This leads to the complaint of some parents to their child's pediatrician that their two- or three-year-old engages in hiding his or her "business" around the house. This behavior is usually easily remedied with the institution of the disapproving mommy or daddy face with the standard "No! No!" proclamation.

Of greater potential concern from a psychiatric standpoint is that if the parents make too big or deal over #2, the child may develop the perception that his #2, beyond being very valuable, also doesn't smell, an attitude that generally doesn't pan out well in later life. Women have often thanked me for this insight, commenting that they now realize that the mother of the man in their life clearly made much too big a deal and fuss over his BMs, so as a result he still behaves like his shit doesn't stink!

The other side of the coin is the condemnation, humiliation approach. This situation often plays out when the child and parent are in a public place, like the mall, and the child has an "accident." The harsh parental response is something like "Oh boy! Now you've done it! Got a load in your pants, aye! Whew! Dude! Do you smell or what?! Everyone knows what you did! How could you do this to your mommy and daddy?"

Despite and in spite of this emotionally harsh approach to toilet training, this child will eventually get out of diapers. But the emotional tag to his or her subconscious, internalized self-face may well be very negative. Where the praised and encouraged child will literally jump for joy and the internalized self-face becomes "what a good boy or good girl I am," the shamed child will internalize "what a bad child I am and what a disappointment I am to my mommy and daddy." This experience is formatted into the individual's mind, and they constantly worry about accidents and other sources of embarrassment or humiliation.

Of course, accidents in later life are not occurrences in your pants, at least I hope not in your case. They take the form of the anxiety or fear that you have forgotten, overlooked, or disregarded something that will have disastrous, personally humiliating consequences later on for sure. To the extreme, these children grow up with high levels of anticipatory anxiety that drives them to take every possible precaution to avoid accidents. They become overly neat and organized, never being able to rest until everything is in the right place or every personal activity is planned out or organized to perfection. They become obsessed with PDAs and checklists. They lack totally or tend to shun any spontaneity or outside-the-box thinking or behaviors in their lives. They will even develop all kinds of rituals to ward off the impending sense of doom.

Where malexperience in the oral phase can portend the most serious of psychiatric decompensations or regressions—a psychotic episode—malexperience in this phase can lead to ingrained personality traits or, at the extreme, personality disorders. Although not as serious as the psychoses, these disorders can nonetheless be very disabling and severely distressing to the individual or to those who have to live with her or him.

Excessively punitive parenting can result in high to extreme levels of anxiety or worrying. This emotional discomfort is often defended against with extreme orderliness or set patterns of behavior—compulsions—from which there can be no acceptable variation or deviation. Early on this often is seen as the worrisome child who has to do things in such a certain way or they will become extremely upset. The child is driven by "rituals" as a mechanism to decrease anxiety and maintain emotional control. In adults this can progress into a full-blown Obsessive-Compulsive Disorder (OCD). Once again, first-born children generally must live through the brunt of their parents' inexperience in child rearing or their parental anxiety about the quality of the job they are doing with their baby. Expectations are often too high and anxiety equally so. In addition to these newly experienced emotional memory tags to the mommy and daddy face, the baby now tags its own face with an anxiety tag, becoming a lifelong believer in Murphy's Law—if it can go wrong, it surely will; any idiot can clearly see that the glass is half empty!

At the other end of the spectrum are the children who are never shown the basic concept of right and wrong, so that essentially they grow up with no anxiety or bad feeling. These children can developmentally become, in adolescence, what is known as Oppositional Defiant Disorder (ODD); if left with no therapy or intervention, they can eventually, as adults, exhibit antisocial behavior patterns, having no conscience or superego restraints against violating the space and rights of others. These antisocial personality disordered people, in effect, shit on the world and everyone in it, and feel no guilt about their actions and the resultant consequences of their behavior whatsoever.

As you can now see, developmental phases and the resultant unconscious "emotional memory," conscious memory, and feelings and behavior patterns are all the result of the child's interaction and relatedness to its environment overlaying their genetic inheritance. At every phase the increments on the scale are infinite; therefore, the number of emotional faces, others and own, with the associated emotional tagging is also infinite. That is why psychiatric diagnoses are not nor can they be rigidly precise, and of necessity must be more fluid and inclusive in order to encompass the most people within the rubric of a specific psychiatric syndrome or diagnostic category. That's why I analogize human beings to snowflakes. Each and every human being has his or her own unique genetic makeup and developmental experiences, even identical twins; as a result, like an individual snowflake they are all totally unique. But while each individual snowflake is unique, they are still part of the larger group—snow.

Developmental experience at the extremes would logically result in extremes of personality development. Keep in mind that human behavior is neither good nor bad, just human behavior. Although one could see Antisocial Personality Disorder as bad, consider that juxtaposed and even somewhat overlapping is Passive Aggressive Personality Disorder.

Although infuriating most often to those in authority, in particular parents, passive aggressive behaviors as mentioned earlier have accomplished great good through the behaviors of humans like Gandhi and Dr. Martin Luther King Jr. Therefore, what Tsaoist wisdom have we learned from all this and can appropriately apply?

To my therapist brethren, never forget the uniqueness of each person you are working with. Remember that this phase of development results in an internalized, emotionally tagged self-face that is both somewhat conscious but to a much greater degree unconscious. Anxiety, its modulation or its resolution, is the driving psychological force in play here. It is what drives the particular externally exhibited behavior. Therapy focused on behavior modification, cognitive behavior therapy (CBT), or similar experiential therapies or approaches may be more effective than traditional talking therapy since much of this developmental process occurs, as in the oral phase, when the child has little facility with language and, as in the foregoing period of development, more of what is remembered is emotional rather than literal.

As with the first developmental phase, seriously debilitating pathologic outcomes can occur. One should, whether therapist or patient, once again consider medication as an adjunctive and important addition to the overall treatment plan. As when faced with a psychotic "me versus not me" breakdown, an antipsychotic or so-called "chemical ego" should be considered; when addressing the core, often emotionally paralyzing anxiety of personality disorders, you should consider adding an "anxiolytic," a minor tranquilizer to make more complete a comprehensive treatment regimen.

In the case of psychosis some of the newer "chemical egos," like Abilify, Geodon, and Seroquel, are quite safe and effective with significantly fewer side effects and less potential for long-term adverse events than similar medications that have gone before them.

To specifically address anxiety there are also many medication alternatives. Over time, the most effective pharmacologic agent for stopping panic attacks, anxiety so great and overwhelming that you believe you are going to die or totally lose your mind, is Xanax (alprazolam) despite its potential for abuse and dependence. It is the one medication that within minutes, without putting a person to sleep or seriously impairing overall functioning, can effectively stop a panic attack.

Of potentially equal effectiveness in the long term, without offering any real immediate relief from a panic attack, is the group of antidepressant medications called the selective serotonin reuptake inhibitors (SSRIs). Although this class of drugs is generally better known for its antidepressant effects, it has, over time, proven to be very effective anxiolytics, offering a longer-term effect on decreasing overall anxiety levels and some prophylaxis against the occurrence and intensity of future panic attacks. This group of drugs includes Prozac, Zoloft, Celexa, and Lexapro.

Research published by the British in 2006 has shown that moderate-term use of fluoxetine hydrochloride (Prozac) can actually stimulate new nerve growth, "neurogenesis," that can result, as a consequence of the increased number of serotonergic neurons, in a potentially longer term or permanent improvement in anxiety and mood levels. These results indicate that the moderate prescription of this SSRI for just twelve months and compliance to the prescription of such may potentially be in some way "curative"! This scientific research adds even more credence to the belief and concept that chronic stress, anxiety, or severe psychological trauma can alter brain structure and function negatively. It follows logically that good emotional experience and/or therapy including medication can possibly reverse those pathologic cerebral changes.

Once again you have already been through this experiential, developmental time, and your internalized, emotionally tagged self-face is well established whether good or bad, positive or negative. Like the recommended quiet time to remember the good stretches of life's highway, at a separate time take an honest look at yourself, saying in effect, "Mirror, mirror on the wall, what is my inner emotional face after all?" Is the glass always half empty? Does Murphy's Law always prevail? Are you obsessed with and continuously anxious about life's accidents? If your self-face looks like this in the mirror of reality, then seriously consider professional help. You can make positive change! It really is possible!

Armed with this knowledge—and hopefully in this instance

knowledge is truly power—that your own emotional face may indeed be scarred beyond hope or therapeutic intervention, you can at the very least make a difference for your future children, or grandchildren. Teach them right from wrong in a positive, loving way. Protect them from the hurts, dangers, and "owies" of life. In order to accomplish this you will have to expend a great deal of both time and effort. It will take a commitment of love to keep your cool while teaching your children the rudiments of right and wrong. It will all be worthwhile in the long run when your child grows up with solid values and experiences less anxiety, with another emotional tag to the memory of the mommy and daddy face that is positive versus potentially negative, punitive, or neglectful.

At this stage the child does the right thing because he or she is consistently monitored. In time, your child can internalize the value system that you have gifted to them. Early on the pattern is woven into the fabric of your child's psychic makeup. As I have lectured in the past, there are people who obey the law to avoid punishment, people who follow the law because deep down they feel or believe that it is the right thing to do, people who disobey or defy the law openly to effect social change, and people who have no concept of right or wrong and blatantly break the law and violate the rights of others. When you take a good look in the psychological mirror, which self-face or combination of faces really fits you? At least with this information you might be able to raise your children with virtue.

My definition of true virtue is doing the right thing when nobody is looking and when the temptation, drive, or pressure of circumstance to do otherwise is the greatest. Are you or can you be "truly" virtuous? Will your children grow up to be so?

3

Oedipus the King

Now we have traveled together through the first three years of human emotional and physical development. We have completed the oral phase and the baby has some sense of "me versus not me" and has started the lifelong process of formatting in the hard drive of its mind faces with associated emotional memory tags. We have journeyed through the anal phase, where baby has learned the initial concepts of right versus wrong and has emotionally tagged his or her own face. We understand that under extreme emotional or physical duress people can "regress" to these earlier stages emotionally and can exhibit severe personality disordered behaviors or even frank psychosis. We have some understanding of ego function and superego function. It is time to move on and look at the life of Oedipus the King.

Basically, the ancient Greek playwright Sophocles tells the story of Oedipus, the son of the king of Thebes, Laius. The king learns from an oracle that his son will grow up and at some time in the future kill him and ascend the throne of Thebes. The king and his wife, young Queen Jocasta, alarmed by this foretelling, decide to take action to abort the events as foretold.

Laius and Jocasta arrange for a local herdsman to take the baby Oedipus into the wilderness and murder him. A lot of the kids I've worked with over the years think of their parents as not being so different from Laius and Jocasta. The herdsman, unfortunately for the murderously conspiring parents, but luckily for Oedipus, doesn't have it in him to kill the baby. Instead, he abandons the little kid in the wilderness and returns to tell the king and queen that he has done their bidding. Along comes a peasant who finds the abandoned baby and rescues it from the wilderness and takes baby Oedipus to his master, King Polybus of Corinth. Polybus immediately takes a liking to little Oedipus, intuitively sensing his royal lineage, and adopts and raises him as his own son. This proves you can't beat fate, at least not in Greek tragedies! The son grows up to be a strapping young man, and years later he is driving his chariot toward Thebes.

Prophetically, King Laius is driving his chariot out of Thebes in the opposite direction, and they meet, chariot to chariot, at an intersection on the road. Neither is willing to concede the right of way, and the first recorded case of road rage ensues during which Oedipus slays his old man. Having no idea whom he has just killed, Oedipus travels on to Thebes and happens to meet his mother, who looks really good for her age, being relatively young chronologically, having given birth to Oedipus at a very young age.

Since he has missed and longed for his real mommy all along, Oedipus feels a strange attraction to this older woman. He eventually falls in love with her, and they marry. Together they have four children, the most well-known being Antigone. Yuck! Incest!

As the story goes, when the truth finally is revealed, Jocasta is so overwhelmed that she commits suicide. Oedipus, having witnessed and participated in the so-called "primal scene" and wanting to destroy that visual image and any and all memory of it forever, blinds himself by gouging his eyes out! Wow! Sophocles really knew how to express things in a theatrical, metaphorical way!

The truth is that we are basically all psychologically "blind" to seeing or accepting the reality of the "primal scene," that any parents and particularly ours actually engage in or have engaged in sexual intercourse. A recent Family Guy episode demonstrated this phenomenon: Peter and his wife, Lois, are having sex in the bathtub and the two older children, Meg and Chris, happen to walk in while they are engaged in the act. The teenagers openly wonder why their parents are "wrestling" in the tub. This Family Guy episode documents that witnessing parents having sexual intercourse is so psychologically taboo and emotionally overwhelming that Meg and Chris, and all of us humans, are emotionally "blind" to the act and cannot actually bring themselves to see or are driven to misinterpret what was happening right before their very eyes—figuratively speaking, tearing out their eyes as Oedipus did in the Greek tragedy.

Understanding the power of this psychological prohibition, I have often used it to curb sexual acting out by my adolescent patients. After they have been caught in the act or have left evidence around that doesn't need a competent CSI investigator to figure out, like a used condom or other DNA impregnated materials, the initial position generally taken by my teenage patients is that they just "don't get" what the big fuss is all about. So what if they had sex and their parents found out about it. It's, after all, the natural biologic thing to do, and their parents need to get a life and accept that having sexual intercourse between teens goes on all the time. In response to this oft-taken position on the matter, I ask my patients if they believe that "their" parents have ever had sex. The power of the taboo usually initially emerges with their responding that it had to have been at least three times because they have two siblings! I then challenge them, using the principal and irresistible power of thought insertion to therapeutic advantage, if they can visualize their mom and dad naked in bed "getting it on." The usual response is, "No way, man. That's disgusting!" Bingo! Therapeutic intervention! I then clarify that it is equally if not more difficult for parents to see or visualize their children engaged in sexual intercourse. The discovery of a used condom under the bed or on the bathroom floor forces mom to visualize it whether or not she wants to, and believe me, she doesn't want to. You don't want to drive your mother to do what Jocasta eventually did, do you? Using this intervention I have been able to bring about some positive behavioral change in my teenage patients related to this particular area of adolescent sexual behavior.

This is the story line that Sigmund Freud adapted to the developmental time from about three years to seven years of age, calling it the Oedipus phase or the Oedipus complex. Once again, although these psychological phases are presented as separate and discrete entities, one should more realistically and truly see them as rather seamless transitions with considerable overlap in terms of psychological development and emotionally tagged faces. As we pass chronologically through this phase, the self-face continues to differentiate and modify its emotional tagging. It is during this phase that the child transitions from undifferentiated child to a little girl or a little boy. With this gender tag development, the child usually starts to emotionally and behaviorally favor one parent over the other.

Gender differentiation initially starts with toilet training, as it soon becomes obvious to the child that there is an anatomical difference between the sexes. Little boys and little girls can both sit on the potty and defecate, but only boys can stand up and urinate without making a mess of things because they have a "tee tee," or penis, and girls don't. There is a psychological school of thought that says women are really affected by this experience, a phenomenon called "penis envy." Carl Jung dubbed this event as the "Electra complex," postulating that little girls, when they realize they don't have a penis, reason that they must have at some point in time had one but were castrated, and in essence blame and hate their mothers for letting this happen to them. Whoa Nellie! Now there's a psychological theory for you! I'll probably score some points with my feminist readers but may be scorned by my psychoanalytic colleagues when I comment that I don't attribute a lot of weight to this theory, despite the fact that both my daughters tried it at least once, that is to stand up and "pee pee." My now child psychologist daughter reports the same experience for my two granddaughters.

It is my belief that the "envy" is more appropriately reality-based. I believe it is more accurately attributed to the American and the global cultural disadvantage and suppression of women monetarily, socially, and politically—although I do feel progress, albeit slow, has occurred in this area over the years of my lifetime. Unfortunately, despite all the progress, one has to keep in mind that gender bias rears its ugly head early in the developmental years, and it has been long and traditionally practiced for centuries around the world. Gender bias will not go easily or quietly into the night! Just because it won't be easy doesn't in any way mean that change shouldn't eventually happen. Hopefully, those parents who read this book may lead the way in terms of change.

Refocusing on the Oedipus/Electra complexes and the theory of face development, this is the time of psychological maturation that, regardless of whether or not one has a penis, you add another dimension to your internalized and external faces: femaleness or maleness. Parental interaction and attitude, as in the previous phases, logically have an enormous impact. After all, what kind of female or male face do you want your child to ultimately develop? This is once again a foundation or building block phase. Just as the oral phase lays down the cornerstone for the perception of reality that is further defined and redefined over time, and as the anal phase lays down the foundation for the concept of right versus wrong that is eventually developed into a personal morality over time, this phase begins with the earliest awakening to the "I'm a little girl" or "I'm a little boy" reality.

This gender separation actually starts months to years earlier with the mommy face's and daddy face's reaction to the child and its gender. Early on little girls get pink and little boys blue. Little girls get flower, butterfly, and kitten patterns. Little boys get football, baseball, and puppy patterns. These symbols of femininity or masculinity are directly associated with the reinforcing, approving mommy and daddy faces and positive mommy and daddy verbal tones with words like, "What a pretty girl!" "What a handsome boy!" Suddenly words or language starts to carry meaning and feeling. Where it all started with face and the quality of touch and the interaction between parent and child, as language develops the child is able to attach language and concepts to the previously cataloged faces and associated emotional tags. Therefore, what was initially an emotional memory, with the onset of language development the child finds more and more words to label the faces and eventually can literally describe the feelings attached to each cataloged face. What was initially a face with a non-literal emotional tag is now further defined as friendly, happy, sad, angry, etc.

Further related to language development, femaleness and maleness jump out at our children from the storybooks of childhood. Cinderella, Sleeping Beauty, Goldielocks are just a few of the many stories that have been read and loved by so many little girls. Come on now. It's all about, "Mirror, mirror on the wall, who's the fairest of them all?" It's all about the handsome prince searching for and eventually finding the beautiful princess. Then there is the magical kiss. They fall in love and "live happily ever after." You've got to be kidding! It's the happily ever after that's really the killer. Nonetheless, it is the wished-for dream of all the little princesses. As the saying goes, be careful what you wish for! But we'll talk in more detail about this subject later.

Theoretically and in reality, under normal circumstances, during this phase little girls exhibit an almost "in love" relationship with their fathers, and little boys develop a similar feeling toward their mothers. This behavior is readily and clearly observable if one takes the time to look. Where mommy was previously the parent to put the little girl to bed at night, all of a sudden during this phase the little girl insists that her daddy must be the one to tuck her in at night and give her the last good-night kiss. Moms often wonder whether they have developed halitosis or should switch deodorants. However, rejected as they may feel by their daughters, mothers take great comfort in "mommy's little man," the two of them becoming adoringly closer and closer, with her little man reassuringly and repeatedly saying to his mom, "I love you so much."

At this stage children put the parent of the opposite sex up on the proverbial pedestal from which lofty height they are for the most part never toppled during their lifetime and even beyond. Therefore, despite what may be the actual truth about the life of the deceased pedestaled parent, it is difficult at best if not impossible to compete with or criticize a ghost. Keep this in mind whether your role is that of a therapist or partner in a relationship. The strength of the psychological need to continue this idealized memory is almost equivalent to the power of the taboo against seeing or thinking about the primal scene.

In regard to the lofty proverbial pedestal, I would offer the following to my therapist colleagues as well as all those contemplating getting into or who are already in the early stages of a budding relationship or those already engaged in a serious relationship. Generally, if this developmental phase is an extremely bumpy stretch of life's highway, fraught with potholes, hazards, and wrecks, then it logically follows that the next level of psychological dysfunction, the so-called "neuroses," develop.

Neurotic people with all their "hang-ups" ultimately become the bread and butter for the majority of psychotherapists, and they consume the greatest number of sessions for multiple and assorted reasons.

First of all, the child at this stage has started to develop language and establish actual literal memory. Therefore, "talking therapy" becomes by its nature applicable and effective. Second, people suffering with neuroses are the most likely to seek help because they are not comfortable with their own self-face, internal or external, or their self-perception of their maleness or femaleness in the arena of social competence and/or acceptance.

People with maladies related to dysfunction in the earlier developmental phases will demonstrate psychoses or personality disorders, and although they are the ones with the greatest need for therapeutic intervention, they generally believe that they don't really need help. For real! After all, if you are God or Allah, it's just not within the realm of possibility that you might need help. You're much too busy running everybody else's lives and the entire universe! After all, it's a really big-time all-consuming job! Who's got time for therapy with all this clear-cut responsibility on your shoulders?

So in walks this patient to your office or this new person to your personal life. Therapist or not, avoid being initially critical or giving any appearance of being critical of their mommy or daddy, the former if it's a man and the latter if it's a woman. Why beware? Remember that as Oedipus was physically blind, they are more or less and similarly psychologically blind, and pushing for insight and behavioral change too early in the thera-peutic or social relationship will drive patients and/or potential significant others away. So, in this particular instance, follow the adage of "let sleeping dogs lie," at least at the beginning of the relationship.

According to psychological theory, as I've noted earlier, dur-ing this time in a child's life, he or she realizes that you cannot really win over mommy or daddy and get rid of the other parent much as Oedipus and Electra accomplished. By around the age of seven, if this reality is finally accepted by the child, then the psychological process shifts to identification with the parent of the same sex.

The little boy, despite his intense incestuous feelings of love for his mommy and his wish to get rid of his daddy, understands that despite his murderous feelings the battle is a total mismatch, sort of on the order of David and Goliath, except with David hav-ing no slingshot and no available stones! According to this con-cept of the son's "David" situation, the boy develops so-called "castration anxiety." We have already discussed the female side in terms of the Electra complex and "penis envy." If this develop-mental conflict goes unresolved, then the Oedipal boy's internal self-face is painted maleness, but a loser or negative maleness that impairs all future relationships with men, seeing them all as bigger, stronger, more aggressive, and more adequate or ca-pable. This person then goes through his life suffering self-doubt and believing that he can never really be successful, often experi-encing guilt over his secret or openly expressed competitiveness with other men.

This process of development may explain how football has become such an obsession, if you will, with the American male in general. The game serves two purposes. First, men can iden-tify with the aggression that takes place on the field of play without having to engage in any real confrontation or putting themselves in any real physical peril. Second, they can revel in "my" team's victories, the reason why winning teams are such popular choices. After all, who wants to identify with a loser, especially if that's a feeling that you may struggle with within yourself to start with? If you have a need to identify with the losers, then you probably need to start seeing a shrink! This behavior pattern is different from a long-standing commitment to a team secondary to family tradition, residence in a certain city, college affiliation, etc. For example, I certainly don't see the long-suffering fans of the Chicago Cubs as "losers" despite their beloved "Cubbies" being without a World Series win in over a century.

Little girls experience the same dilemma with their mothers, but since there is a lower level of overall physical aggression in women, this confrontation, more likely a battle of words, is generally less traumatic and potentially more easily resolved, although not always so.

Nonetheless, if you were to ask little girls who they would most want to marry in the future, they will very seriously say, with little hesitation, "my daddy." Little boys at this stage, with little prompting say, "When I grow up, I'm going to marry my mommy." It's all so cute and so psychologically predictable. Once again referring to the football example, look at how the players in the National Football League shower material things on and take such good care of their "mommies."

In either case, barring some really strange circumstances, by the end of this phase of development, the child realistically gives up the vast majority of the romance with the opposite-sex parent, at least on an everyday conscious level and decides to be like the parent of the same sex, a psychological process referred to as "identification." But, as Anna Freud pointed out, and I humbly agree, no one really comes through this phase unscathed, meaning that to a greater or lesser degree we're all a little bit neurotic and have hang-ups! Ah! Job security for shrinks!

As noted earlier, the psychological, behavioral sequelae to an abnormal experience or trauma in the two previous developmental phases are severe behavioral and/or mental dysfunction, where the patient has a misperception about the world and human relatedness. Where the former have a struggle with the external world and overall reality, the struggle related to the Oedipus phase is more internal, more a conflict within and against the self. So accepting that Anna Freud was right, we all come away from this phase with some issues or hang-ups. These issues or hang-ups are often experienced as repeatedly getting involved in relationships that are going nowhere or which are frankly destructive to both parties involved. These destructive relationships can be interpersonal or career related. People in these situations may blame it on others, but more often than not secretly blame themselves. Unfortunately, these neuroses-plagued people seldom take the proverbial bull by the horns and make a proactive decision to swim against the current and change their oft-repeated self-defeating pattern of behavior although these are exactly the people who can truly get the most out of psychotherapy.

So, enjoy your therapy sessions, but please also consider the institution of some of my Tsaoism suggestions about life's highway and positive thought insertion, self-initiated brainwashing if you will. You can do it!

Now I will take a look at a statistical phenomenon in psychiatry before moving on to the next chapter. It has been well documented and widely published that more women seek counseling or therapy than men, indicating that women are more neurotic than men or, at least may be more self-aware and, therefore, seek professional help more frequently than men. With the more serious diagnoses like schizophrenia and bipolar disorder, the ratio of women to men requiring some sort of intervention is basically 50/50. So why are there more neurotic women? Is it gender bias? It has been postulated, mostly by women I might add, that this phenomenon is the result of women having to put up with men and their bad behaviors! However, I offer this alternative view for your consideration.

Statistically, 50 percent or more of American marriages end in divorce, a truly sad but significant number. The number of injured and dysfunctional families grows significantly beyond 50 percent when you add in the large number of marital separations, real or emotionally de facto.

In divorce situations, magistrates and judges generally award the physical custody of the children to the mother. What an award! For real, now the mother has to serve the role of both parents often with significantly less available resources and significantly more stress. The situation is not in any major way dissimilar with separations. The real issue here is the Oedipus/ Electra complex. As portrayed by Sophocles, actually winning the Oedipus struggle—incest—has potentially dire consequences. With the stroke of the pen, the judge makes the son the winner and the daughter the loser! Remember, the little boy always secretly wanted mommy all for himself. The little girl similarly wanted her daddy! Although both children suffer loss with divorce, the little girl suffers the greater psychological loss. It is a loss of time as a result of limited visitation. It is a loss of that special love and security from daddy and the closeness to him. It is a loss of opportunities to progress and develop normally through this psychological stage of development. In effect, these girls spend the rest of their lives searching for the daddy they never got to experience. Obviously, the potential emotional impact of the loss will correlate to the age of the child at the time of the family breakup. As a result, they generally will experience their self-face as incomplete and clearly negative, resulting in low self-esteem, low self-confidence, depression, anxiety, and attention-seeking, acting-out behaviors. It renders these girls, because of their emotional neediness, as easy prey for predators of all kinds.

Should they become victims of predation, and so many of them often are, they are so seriously further traumatized and damaged by the combined events that they are more often than not crippled emotionally for life. After more than forty years in practice I have lost count of the number of teenage girls who, after they have over time been able to develop a trusting, working relationship with me, have gained an understanding and insight into why they have "put out" sexually so frequently during their young lives. They all tearfully understand that this so-called promiscuous behavior is driven by an unrequited need for someone, anyone, to spend time with them, pay attention to them, and say, "I love you." They honestly report that most often they don't really get anything physically, in terms of true pleasure or orgasm, out of sexual intercourse itself, but intuitively or consciously they know that the offering of sex will garner the attention and time that they so desperately want and need from men, what they most deeply have an insatiable psychological hunger for and an emotional void they are desperately driven to fill.

An additional and compounding factor for the daughters of divorce is the general attitude of their custodial mothers, implied or openly expressed about their estranged father during the separation process, the divorce, and the time thereafter.

Understandably, dependent on the circumstances driving the marital breakup, mothers almost always sustain negative feelings ranging from disappointment to frank hatred toward their daughter's father, the latter feeling the most usual emotion experienced and expressed. This opinion is communicated over and over again—that the girl's father is a no-good, no-account person, this being on the milder end of the spectrum as maternal feelings go. Mothers, driven by their own hurt and anger, forget that they are smearing their daughter's father, the man with whom she was supposed to experience her first true, ideal, and unconditional love.

Remember the irresistible power of thought insertion? You can see its potential psychological destructiveness come into play here for the daughter in this all too frequently played-out life drama.

It has been my experience that a constant, supportive, and loving grandfather can be very helpful to granddaughters in this particular and unfortunately sad situation.

It has become abundantly clear that this is often why young girls are brought to treatment or older women seek treatment, suffering emotionally as a result of this lost relationship with their fathers and the emotional traumas that are sure to follow. Even more tragic, as I've already noted, are the younger girls who beyond this early trauma have then later been victimized and traumatized by predators, being easily identified by said predators due to their extreme and obvious emotional neediness.

The good news is that the former group, the girls who have not been terribly victimized, respond well to therapy. In essence, using positive thought insertion during sessions, as everybody has something positive about themselves or their life experiences, and instructing my patients on how to use this method themselves outside of our formal sessions, has proven to be a very effective part of a comprehensive therapeutic intervention.

Being a steady, supportive persona in their life is of positive therapeutic benefit. These women can sense it when you are knowledgeable, experienced, and have a true understanding of their emotional struggle. It may be that since a good percentage of the neurosis for women is based on a lack of time or a total absence of a father figure, a "fatherly" male therapist may be statistically more effective in such treatment situations, not to say that a woman therapist, armed with this insight and understanding cannot also be very effective. As one of my colleagues, Dr. Pierre Golpira, insightfully noted, these women particularly need a man therapist who won't take advantage of the so-called transference or the feelings of the woman patient to fulfill any of his own personal psychological or, even worse, physical sexual needs. It's the last thing a woman in this state of mind needs, to have her therapist become another predator in her life! Because of the gross violation of trust and the potential for immeasurable psychological damage, you can see why there is such strong censure against any therapist for engaging in such behavior.

4

Drill Instructor

Much of the previous psychiatric/psychological literature has labeled the development between the Oedipal phase and the beginning of adolescence as "latency," implying quiescence and behavioral, emotional peace and tranquility during these particular formative years. It may be true that there is little behavioral upheaval after the passion of Oedipus and before the emotionally perfect storm called adolescence. But, if oral, anal and Oedipal are the cornerstone and foundation of psychological development, then latency is the framing of the human psychological house.

During this developmental time the child is formatting a social face, developing an initial concept of self outside of family with a great deal of input and feedback from within the family, at least initially. The child is formulating some idea of where he or she fits or doesn't fit into the greater scheme of things. There is further development of girlness/femininity and boyness/masculinity.

This all starts with day care or preschool, pre-kindergarten or kindergarten. The child with the occurrence of this event is forced to move from the comfort, safety, and familiarity of home and all its supportive and loving faces to a world that is new, vast, and unfamiliar, populated with so many new and unfamiliar faces! It is a daunting and often frightening task. This oft-overwhelming experience is documented by the manner in which the child behaves when being "dropped off" for the first time. How many mothers have endured and suffered through the traumatic experience of leaving their little one in the care of a stranger for the first time. Some children, the exception to the rule and usually not a first-born child, blissfully embrace this new experience while the majority generally exhibit varying degrees of separation anxiety, from hesitantly moving toward the smiling, verbally encouraging face, the short journey punctuated by multiple pauses and furtive glances back at the mommy face, to a full-blown meltdown during which the child becomes a vice-like attachment to one of mommy's legs, accompanied by wailing and copious tears.

What is a mother to do in this situation? Assuming that you have done due diligence and checked out the day care or the pre-K staff and found only glowing references, and not even the slightest hint of a connection to anyone listed on the national sex offender list posted on the Internet, the best plan of action is to pry your child loose, turn his or her care over to the sympathetically smiling lady, beat a hasty retreat, and exit the scene. Rest assured that in today's world of instant communication, should your child be totally unwilling or incapable of clearing this developmental hurdle in the separation individuation process, your cell phone will serve as the means by which you will be summoned back to pick up your child if this experience is too much for your child to deal with at this time in his or her life.

Consider a number of things you can do to prepare your child for this inevitable and developmentally important transition. Believe it or not, mom, sharing your child's early upbringing with your mother or mother-in-law affords the child the opportunity to interact with other faces that are consistent, loving, and caring but are not the mommy face. If your mother or mother-in-law is not readily available, find another mom with a child close to yours in age and get together regularly for "play dates," allowing the children to interact to whatever age-appropriate degree. Share the caretaking of both children; this way your child will experience an initially unfamiliar face as an ultimately positive thing, a face other than the mommy's that now has an emotionally positive tag.

For the child who could not initially make the first separation, give it a little time, then, no pun intended, take baby steps—like stay with your child at the daycare facility for the entire scheduled time, weaning down gradually until the separation process is complete.

Remember that at the end of Oedipus, your child has realistically given up on getting rid of the parent of the same sex and has moved to a position of identifying with and taking on the personality and behavioral characteristics of the parent of the same sex. In effect, the girls say, "Since I really can't get rid of my mom; and since there must have been something about mom that captured dad's affection, love, and devotion; and since I love and want to please my daddy, then I will become as much like mommy as humanly possible." The reverse holds true for the boys. It is during this time, dad that you become your child's first significant role model, good, bad, or indifferent! Think about it.

During this time your children watch your every move. They study your every expression. They hang onto your every word. And speaking of hanging on to every word, I mean every word! Especially, the explicatives! In fact, this phenomenon occurs even at an earlier age but is solidified throughout latency.

I vividly recall an episode that occurred more than thirty-five years ago when my younger daughter, Sam, was just three years of age. I had come home from work and was chatting with my wife as we prepared dinner together. I couldn't help but notice little Sam busily playing with "Dressy Bessy," a doll created with various tasks of dressing and undressing. This particular evening Sam was working diligently on the buttons. I watched her button Bessy up, but the buttons when she finished the task were misaligned. Showing some level of frustration, she unbuttoned Bessy and made a second attempt. Unfortunately, she overcompensated and this time the buttons were misaligned the opposite way. When she realized this, while holding Bessy up for inspection, she disgustingly blurted out, "Shit!" I immediately turned to my wife who, quite red-faced, said, "Sorry, honey. I might have let that slip once." But, even beyond the expletives, and surely more important, is the fact that children hang on to all your words, expressions, and behaviors. Do you have religious beliefs and actually practice such? Are you prejudiced and bigoted or open-minded and accepting of all people, their customs, and beliefs? Do you really accept that the environment needs protection and practice preservation and conservation? Do you smoke cigarettes, drink excessively, or use drugs? Your children will model these negative self-destructive behaviors sooner or later. Trust me. This is your opportunity to mold your child into an adult, possibly and hopefully even a better adult than you yourself are, someone you can truly be proud of.

As I've noted already, during this time little girls become smaller versions of their mothers and boys smaller versions of their fathers. They mimic and integrate into their own persona all that they see, hear, and feel—everything, the total experience! Therefore, as a parent you will reap what you sow. Should your child experience you as tense or easygoing, happy or depressed, loving or angry, emotionally open or closed, affectionate or cold and distrusting, this becomes the emotional foundational framework for his or her eventual adult personality characteristics. So what role model are you going to present for your children to emulate? How do you handle responsibility? How do you handle the frustrations of life, small or great? Can you accept victory and defeat and treat them as equals? If you demonstrate that keeping your cool, and that persistence and effort result in success, then the acorn literally won't fall far from the oak, and your child will grow up to be a strong individual. On the other hand, if you demonstrate, when faced with adversity, an emotional meltdown and easily then give up, what does your child learn? Do you see my point here?

This is a good time to talk about discipline. Children need it! They have already learned from "No! No!" that there are things they shouldn't do, but now is a time to learn about what right and wrong really means and how to behave appropriately.

Hopefully, you have never engaged in felonious assault against your child! Have you ever struck your child out of frustration or anger? How is that any different from striking another adult out of frustration or anger? In fact, it is really a greater crime against a child since it is such a physical mismatch, with the child being essentially defenseless.

Despite the physical damage inflicted, the psychological damage is clearly greater, having potential long-term negative emotional fallout long after any physical hurt has been healed. Here is the daddy or mommy face that exhibits rage, the daddy or mommy face that has been and is most important to the child, and whom he or she most wants to please, an angry face spewing out angry words, expressing and demonstrating rageful emotion. The hands that have held and loved now inflicting pain! How can the child know that mommy or daddy, in his or her angry state of mind, will stop short of killing them? They don't! In fact, police records, court proceedings, and news reporting abound with stories of children being killed at the hands of their very own parents! This dichotomy is understandably overwhelming and incomprehensible to the child, shaking the basic foundation of his or her basic trust, leading to potentially lifelong elevated anxiety levels, trust issues, and debilitating relationship problems.

So, what is a parent to do? It is a known psychological truth that the people in our lives in whom we have the most emotional investment, "love" if you will, can frustrate and anger us the very most. Thus explains the high incidence of domestic violence between adults and, in this instance, against children. My advice to parents is to never lay a hand on your child in a state of anger or rage. First of all, it's against the law! Second, it is extremely psychologically damaging! I have worked with many, many parents for whom corporal punishment has led them to run afoul of the law, resulting occasionally in jail time but always resulting in having to live their lives for many years under the watchful eye of Child Protective Services (CPS). Some parents I have worked with have stated, in their own defense, that as children they themselves were spanked or switched, and they are none the worse for wear from this experience. I usually counter by pointing out that back then it may not have been against the law, but now it is; therefore, they have been legally identified as the aggressor and have been referred to me by CPS, the courts, or their own lawyers. I point out the clear and well-established correlation between people who have been beaten as children and the high incidence of carrying this damaging legacy forward.

I believe that the psychological damage of corporal punishment is self-evident. On the other hand, it is the nature of children to act up and act out. So how can parents manage effective discipline so that their child can learn self-discipline?

The point to note here is that without discipline, the child will never learn self-discipline. In my experience a child without self-discipline will have a very difficult, if not impossible, task to become successful in later life! I've seen this scenario play out countless times in my forty-plus years as a physician and psychiatrist. I have witnessed many children with above-average IQs, above-average physical talent, above-average artistic talent, above-average everything never come close to fulfilling their potential in any of these areas. It is a loss they and their families tragically have to live with for the rest of their lives.

Once you accept that physical aggression and the inflicting of pain have significant, negative psychological impact and sequelae, the answer for effecting good parenting in this area is consistent non-assaultive interaction with the child over time. It all starts with "No! No!"—the most basic concept of right versus wrong developed from the time of Elmo through latency to a greater understanding of why certain behaviors are acceptable or not acceptable. Ingrained in this is a sense of what is fair versus unfair. That is the great task and challenge of parenting at this phase of development. During this time the child is the most malleable physically and emotionally and is generally driven by a great need to please his or her parents.

Boy, does that change in adolescence! And well it should! Where in latency we teach our children right versus wrong and fair versus unfair, in the next phase we should actually foster and encourage the challenging of conventional wisdom. Boy, do I suffer having apparently done a good job with my own children, when during family get-togethers my daughters and their husbands debate politics with their mother and me. I do believe that sociopolitical thinking in humans is like military marching, a left/right experience. When a person is young and filled with idealistic vigor, one tends to be socially liberal or left. Over time, with life's experiences, that right, more conservative foot will tend to come forward. Even in my late sixties my feet are still basically even. Maybe in my seventies my right foot will protrude a little more.

I am reminded of one of my final experiences of residency training at the Institute of Pennsylvania Hospital. Just before graduation, I was called down for my exit interview with Dr. J. Martin Meyers, the director of the psychiatric residency and fellowship programs, a very learned and precise man whom I had come to respect greatly for his knowledge, wisdom, and values. When I entered his office, it was late afternoon, and Dr. Meyers was standing at the window behind his large wooden desk. He appeared to be peering through the half-open wooden Venetian blinds with his hands held gently together behind him.

"Dr. Tsao, do you believe in God?" It was a rhetorical question as he continued before I could formulate any sort of answer. "When I was a younger man, I was convinced that there was no God. I believed that we humans are the masters of our own life's ship and could chart a course for our own lives, and for some of us even the future of humanity. But now as I travel through the autumn of my life, I am not so sure. I've started going to church again."

I'm sure we talked about many things that afternoon, but that is my one lasting memory of that final meeting. We are obligated as parents to share with our children a clear concept of right versus wrong and our socio-religious beliefs so that they can further develop, accept, or even reject them totally in the future. I hope that wherever he is now, Dr. Meyers found what he was looking for. I suspect also that my children's political feet will come closer together over time.

Dr. Meyers's life experience elucidated an issue that will emerge in adolescence that I would like to take a look at now. Adolescents generally turn away from religion, even if raised in a very religious family environment. This can be very upsetting to the parents, particularly those of strong personal religious belief. I usually get to work with these kids after their parents have gone to great lengths to get them to "see the truth" of their "evil ways," but it has resulted in minimal to no success at all. When I have finally developed a working relationship with the preteen or adolescent, I usually find out that the child on some level really embraces a lot of what his or her parents have taught but feels obligated to push back against the coercion and blatant pressure of his or her parents. The more the parents push, the harder the adolescent pushes back. This pushing match between adolescent and parent is often just a normal manifestation of the maturational process of separation-individuation and not necessarily a sign of significant mental dysfunction.

There are two factors underlying this behavioral, psychological change. First, as you clearly know or will see and understand in the next chapter, it is part and parcel of normal healthy growing up to rebel to a lesser or greater degree against authority, specifically parental authority. Of course, the rebellion is against any and all authority figures, so parents should avoid taking this rebellion too personally. But, consider this concept: Is there any authority figure, real or imagined, that is bigger or greater than God? Thus explains why God is on the outs during the teenage years.

Second, and of equal if not greater impact, is that if we accept the existence of God, Allah, or another supreme being who sees all and knows all, then for sure we're going to burn in hell or whatever bad place for the things we do or think during our adolescence. Let's get real. Do you really think that any teenager can or wants to accept that there might be someone who can see everything good or bad, especially the bad things that he or she does or the bad things that he or she thinks? Hell, no! For this reason alone, as I've just pointed out, God is definitely on the outs with most teenagers. This may also explain why even adults have similar struggles with their own particular faiths.

Human beings often invoke the name of God or ask divine intervention in times of stress, tragedy, or impending disaster. Could it have been that this was what Dr. Meyers was going through at that time and stage in his life?

During latency is indeed the time and the opportunity to mold your child's internal values system. If he or she doesn't embrace respect for authority, the law, or themselves in terms of a personal value system here, you don't want to face what you are going to have to experience during their adolescent years.

As a former U.S. Naval officer, I can't help but think of the U.S. Marine Corps. The Corps' drill instructors, or "DI's" as they are known, take a raw group of volunteer recruits through a twelve- to thirteen-week experience called "boot camp," where they mold these young women and men into U.S. Marines. What the Corps accomplishes is in essence what you as parents want to accomplish with your children over the first twelve to thirteen years of their lives.

Through intense physical challenge, education, and training, the recruits learn what their bodies are capable of doing, usually much more than they ever dreamed possible. Getting your child involved in sports activities can teach them to appreciate what they are physically capable of accomplishing, probably more than they ever thought possible.

The Corps teaches the recruits to depend on each other, that through teamwork, greater goals can be reached than by any individual's effort alone, that the sum is far greater than all the individual parts combined. They learn and hold to be true the cliché, "There is no 'I' in team," an important value for your child to learn through team sports and similar activities.

The Corps teaches that through adversity and failure you can learn great lessons. From loss or defeat, with analysis, planning, change in action plan, and perseverance there is no goal that cannot be ultimately reached or obstacle overcome.

They learn at the core of their being the meaning of Semper Fi, "forever faithful," no marine ever left behind, a belief carried long after their active duty days, a lasting source of great comfort that another marine will always have your back. In essence, isn't this what you want for your child—strong personal values, physical fitness, perseverance, and a strong sense of commitment to family, no family member left behind?

How does the Marine Corps take a young, undisciplined group of individuals and turn them into a cohesive, goal-directed group? Do they let the recruits choose their own activities and schedule? Do the recruits choose what time to get up in the morning, when to eat meals, when to go to class, when it's lights out and time to be in bed? Is back talk and disrespect even remotely tolerated? I think not! There is an organized, structured daily schedule of vigorous physical and educational activities, each day building upon what was learned the day before. Justice for indiscretions of word or action is swift, causally related, and consistent. Consistent is the meaningful word here. Each day is filled with the drill instructor constantly and relentlessly screaming in each recruit's face, yelling, challenging, exhorting, and most of all encouraging, in effect saying in so many different ways, "Son, you can do it!"

So where the U.S. Marine Corps has just thirteen weeks to change a young person's life, you have thirteen years to reach essentially the same goal with your child.

At the end of boot camp through the "tough love" of their drill instructors and the precisely structured program, those who graduate to become U.S. Marines have learned great self-confidence, a commitment to strong personal values, a belief in teamwork, a commitment to family, a commitment to country, a belief in perseverance and self-discipline, and an enduring respect for authority either civil or religious. If your child has not learned all these things, especially respect for parents, at the end of thirteen years, as a Marine has accomplished after thirteen weeks, you've got a potentially "huge" problem on your hands.

Tens of thousands of my therapy hours over the years have been filled with kids who tragically have not been taught nor do they believe in any of these values. My experience speaks loudly and eloquently to the reality that it is easier to effect positive change in those children and adolescents who have been taught some set of values, good or bad, versus those kids who have, out of neglect, plan, or life's circumstance been left to choose their own schedule and activities. This is not to say that a child cannot develop behavioral problems with very organized, strict, and loving parents. However, psychotherapeutic work is generally much easier and more effective with those young people as, at least, I have some system or framework to work with and from rather than the void of no system of values at all.

The Tsaoism recommendation here is that through this developmental stage of latency you must become a loving parental drill instructor. It will require once again a major commitment of time, understanding, effort, patience, and love. Like the Marine Corps, you will have to establish a schedule. This schedule will be less intense than the Corps' because a good part of the weekdays will be taken up by school and school activities, often the respite that you or your spouse will need in order to muster the strength and commitment to raise your child in the afternoons, evenings, and weekends. As parents you have to be on the same page or as a single parent you must offer this consistency.

Too often there is no plan, and children spend too much time watching television or hooked up to the Internet or another personal electronic device. Do you want your child being raised by and learning about life and life's lessons from television or the Internet? Let's face it: It's easier for parents to let their child while away the hours, and I mean potentially thousands of hours, in the care of and under the mind-numbing, brainwashing influence of these electronic babysitters! These children spend their formative years passively imprinting a distorted, overly dramatic by design, view of life. The "gamers" spend a majority of their waking hours in the "virtual world" rather than in the real world!

In the virtual universe, there is so much fantasy and magic. Your child, in effect, regresses back in terms of psychological function to where he or she is once again the epicenter of the universe, able to magically conjure up all and everything he or she needs to fulfill their wishes for immediate gratification. Does this remind you of what we discussed in chapter I? The virtual experience is just too far removed from real life and real time, the only possible gain being improved hand-eye coordination, maybe. The loss is a comprehensive inability to cope with the realities of life in the real world. This is an addiction of epic proportions that is destroying the physical and psychological fiber of America's children. The lobby of my office is clearly a much more quiet environment overall these days than in the past as most of the young patients are now locked into their portable gaming devices, the exception being the hyperactive kid who hasn't taken his medication and doesn't have such an electronic diversion. Often I have to ask, more often than once I might add, that the particular child please discontinue the use of the electronic device during our session, the reluctance or resistance on the patient's part clearly being the evidence of a pathologic addictive behavior pattern.

Am I saying never buy such devices for your children or never allow them access to television or the Internet? Not at all! Much potential good can come from these resources, but as a loving parental drill instructor, you set the schedule and not your child. Related to all this, I would like to tip my hat to all the parents who consistently stand on the sidelines or up in the stands, cheering wildly or just quietly being there for their children.

First of all, it's worth repeating again that team sports teach a valuable lesson—the major focus of the Marines: there is no "I" in team. I have witnessed my granddaughter Charlotte learn so much about life and herself as she has progressed from pee-wee soccer though U12 Club Travel Select soccer, from a bunch of undisciplined girls and boys all running around helter-skelter trying to kick the ball with no apparent purpose or goal, transformed over time to the current "Aztec Soccer Club," where each girl knows her position and its responsibilities, and they function smoothly as a team with a single-minded purpose: to attack, defend, and ultimately win the game. However, I must honestly admit that the little ones and their apparent aimless play is still dear to my heart; I remember fondly the little goalkeeper being more intent on picking dandelion flowers than defending the goal net.

It is most important to understand that the little ones always play seeking the approving gaze of one or both parents, the approving mommy or daddy faces. Charlotte's team didn't always win. In fact, they lost more than they won in the early going. One of my colleagues, Dr. John Phocas, wisely noted that we learn so much more from defeat than from victory, that we seldom analyze, change, or grow as a result of a win. And so it was for Charlotte, that after a loss her daddy would spend one-on-one time with her fulfilling his role as the loving parental drill instructor. The first goal was to wipe away the tears and then to analyze why the "Clamors," her team at that early age, had lost and what part my granddaughter played in that defeat. The usual message was that the Clamors didn't play effectively as a team. The result of all this is a twelve-year-old who has learned so much about herself and gained so much self-confidence in her physical capabilities, having become an integral part of a group of girls that can accept defeat and rejoice in victory together as a "team."

You cannot, in any way, shape, or form, get this from virtual soccer. My granddaughter is one of the more petite girls on the team, but she can run with control and manipulate the ball with equal proficiency with either foot. She is in a word "tenacious"! It has been such a joy to see Charlotte and her daddy practicing her soccer skills in the backyard. It's a priceless time of sharing between a daughter and her father. There's just no way your child or any other child can experience this in the virtual world! No possible way! I can't emphasize enough how important it is to be the drill instructor parent, always in your child's face pushing the idea and belief that he or she "can do it," can truly succeed. Beyond teaching your child the emotional skills to best deal with life's failures and successes equally, even more importantly, you are demonstrating by word and action that you truly love him or her. That's right, that you truly love your child! In this case your actions represent and establish "I love you" far beyond any words you can say.

When children are little, they constantly seek out the mommy or daddy face in the crowd; as they grow up, they may appear to scan the crowd less intensely, but they'll always know if you're there or not! I'm always reminded and impressed that Oedipus and Electra are never buried and gone from the previous developmental stage. If you watch the reactions of collegiate basketball championship teams, the women, when on camera, say "I love you, daddy!" and the boys, "I love you, mom!" For young professional woman golfers and tennis players, it's all about their fathers. Human behavior is once again so, so predictable and in a sense wonderfully so!

However, sports is far from everything this phase is all about. It can be about talking and going for walks. It can be about getting something to eat together, going to the movies, going to religious services. It's all about being aware of what your child is doing in school, reading for fun together, and helping with homework. I am reminded that a few years back as my wife and I were downsizing to a senior condominium from the home where we had raised our daughters, Sam our youngest, came home to help us pack up and move. During the process she found *The Supermarket Mystery* and *The Hobbit*. The supermarket storybook was worn, tattered, and scribbled upon as it was her favorite childhood story and read together innumerable times. The Hobbit was also well-worn but not scribbled upon as it was shared when Sam was older. With joyful tears in her eyes, she asked if she could have these cherished books because they were associated with so many positive and loving memories and had reached Velveteen Rabbit condition as the result of so many readings and equally as many close loving times spent together. Early on Sam learned from both her parents that reading was a good and valuable activity. She experienced reading as fun and immensely fulfilling emotionally. She eventually became a Magna graduate of Duke University!

Similarly, when I was a child, my immigrant father, even after a long hard day's work, would sit at the kitchen table while my brother and I did our homework. Maybe it's a Chinese/Asian thing, but the message was that education was a good and honorable thing. My brother eventually became a lawyer and I a physician. My mom and dad also made non-school learning fun. Despite spending my early years growing up in a third-story walkup apartment in Harlem, good behavior was continuously rewarded by trips to the Museum of Natural History, the planetarium, and the zoo.

At that time in my life I believed that my father could do anything. Although he grew up in China and didn't understand American sports, he alternatively introduced my brother and me to clamming by using our feet, crabbing, and fishing, always followed by a delicious meal from the fruits of our endeavors. I can still see in my mind's eye our first Heddon fiberglass fishing rods and the spool-type fishing reels that my father brought home as birthday gifts for my brother and me. To this very day I still find real joy in fishing, and probably related to this experience emotionally, I still prefer a spool-bait caster type of reel! Give the gift of time and experience to your child, and it truly is a gift that keeps on giving and will have a positive impact for life. My father was my hero.

Like all boys my age, my father wasn't my only hero. Growing up in America I learned to play and love baseball, "America's game." Living in New York, I, of course, grew up rooting for the New York Yankees. Since I couldn't get the hang of fielding ground balls, I played the outfield. The Yankees outfield at that time consisted of Gene Woodling, Mickey Mantle, and Hank Bauer. When I was lucky enough to leave the concrete environment of my neighborhood and take in a game at "The House That Ruth Built," I would focus my attention on my Yankee hero, and it wasn't the Mick! It was Hank Bauer, the right fielder. He was my hero because he had served America as a U.S. Marine, and despite not having quite the pure physical talents of the other two, he succeeded because of hard work, perseverance, hustle, knowledge, and love of the game, plus lots of true grit. I admired and identified with Hank, and he never let me down as a role model. That's the point: He never let me down!

Today's sports, entertainment, and other public role models have a major impact on the minds, values, and ultimately the behavior of our children. They have a "responsibility," a big responsibility, for how they behave! I appreciated the playing ability of Sir Charles Barkley as a professional basketball player, but I cannot disagree more with his proclamation, "I'm not no role model." Like it or not, he has been and will continue to be such as are all high-profile public figures.

Particularly poignant and painful to me at this time is the desecration of the game that I have loved so much over these many years. As a child, the "Black Sox Scandal" only affected me as my Uncle Lou talked about it. I certainly didn't experience it personally. However, I remember vividly the hullabaloo as Roger Maris approached and passed "The Babe's" single-season home run record. I literally jumped for joy when "Hammerin' Hank," a wisp of a man, hit number 715 and fulfilled the legacy and promise of Jackie Robinson.

And now this abomination: "The Steroid Era." I was initially numb in disbelief, then immensely saddened for "the game," and finally so angry that the so-called heroes of this generation are nothing more than a bunch of cheaters who have misled our children, demonstrating by their narcissistic behavior that it is okay to cheat and then, even worse, arrogantly lie about it! What awful role models!

There must be justice for the sake of this generation of children! Our children need and deserve better heroes! Maybe the Bonds's base-ball, now residing in Cooperstown, marked clearly with an asterisk is a small measure of justice. Always keep in mind that despite the ruckus and media circus surrounding these celebrated public figures, the most important role models are those who are up close and per-sonal on a daily basis, the parents themselves and the others who I consistently interact with the developing child in real time.

Be that as it may, despite good drill instructor parenting and pos-itive role models and heroes, your children will act up and test the limits of behavior and your patience as a parent. We have already seen that corporal punishment is ineffective at best and terribly de-structive at worst. The word here is "restriction." This usually means confinement to one's room without toys or other potential diversions. This process obviously starts long before latency, but it is clearly so-lidified up to and throughout the teenage years.

Earlier in latency the parent is clearly larger, stronger, and hope-fully smarter than the child. Although I cannot remember the specif-ics of the behavior code violation by my younger daughter, she was banished to her room until she had accepted and understood that what she had done was wrong, and admitted such to her mom and me. I walked her to her room and closed the door. Well, Sam, as is often the case with second children, was more stubborn and willful, and within a minute or less she was back out of her room. When I told her to return to her room, she, with a defiant countenance, said, "No!" Realizing my responsibility, I gently but firmly gathered up my little one, squirming and crying as she was, carried her to her room, and closed the door. Since we had no locks on the bedroom doors, nor would I recommend locking a child in her room in any case, within seconds Sam was coming out again. I intercepted her and returned her to her room, clearly stating that she was to stay there until she settled down and had time to think about what she had done. I also stated that I would be sitting sentinel outside her door in order to enforce the restriction.

Just as I finished explaining the situation in detail, I heard the crescendo of music and the voice of Howard Cosell hawking Monday Night Football's presentation of the clash between bitter rivals the Dallas Cowboys and the Washington Redskins. What a bind! I really wanted to watch the game, but there was Sam to deal with. The cliché "no pain, no gain" applies not only to football and other sports, but oft times too frequently to parenting also. In this case, I missed the first quarter sitting at Sam's door and enforcing her restriction. Sam never really had a behavior problem, I believe in some way because she always knew that her parents truly loved her and would enforce reasonable consequences as warranted.

Early on for the youngster the enforced separation and wish to please motivates the child to think and consider changing his or her behaviors. You must be consistent and enforce the separation over time in order to effect good parenting. Later in development, when separation no longer carries as much impact, then you can restrict access to the child's favorite things: games, friends, TV, the Internet, cell phone, car keys, etc.

With boys, in their teens, the power of the car keys is huge. For girls, the cell phone carries the big impact. The question then becomes how long should a restriction last? Shorter periods of time when the child is younger and longer as they age, without going "too" far, is a good rule of thumb. My experience as a psychiatrist has elucidated that longer than a week is clearly counterproductive. Such long restrictions inevitably turn into a battle with the original reason for the disciplinary action long forgotten or significantly distorted.

An example from later adolescence involved my older daughter, Susan. I should first point out that Susan was basically a wonderful daughter and still is. She made straight A's in school, loved to read, was thoughtful, and engaged in few behavioral indiscretions, at least that I am aware of. The rule of the Tsao house was that if you came home late without a legitimate excuse, associated with no attempt to call, you were not going out socially or otherwise the very next weekend. Indeed, Susan did come home late once and was informed and reminded of this established consequence, which she readily accepted until she realized, a day or so later, that she had tickets to a concert the very next weekend! She then tried to negotiate and, boy, could she negotiate! If she could go to the concert, she would trade for the next weekend or two. No deal! Susan gave the tickets to friends. During her restriction we had some discussion about how much her parents really loved her and worried when she was late and didn't call, how important it was to me that she be responsible, and we never had a problem with tardiness again. This particular episode makes the point, once again, that as parents you must be consistent and follow through with what you say—and not just consequences for behavioral mistakes, but all commitments or promises that you have made to your children.

This may be one factor in why children of divorce tend to be so much less self-disciplined. They seldom experience their mom and dad working together as a team. In fact, it's usually quite the opposite.

Assuming now that you have succeeded in being a loving drill instructor parent—I never said nor is it written anywhere that it would be easy—the good news is that the basic foundation and structure of your child's psychological health—his or her self-face and perception of other faces—is solid and well-established and for the most part positive. The bad news is that you're still facing adolescence!

Before we move on to the next chapter I want to discuss a popular and controversial subject: ADD/ADHD. I have spoken to thousands of physicians, nurse practitioners, and mental health professionals about this malady for literally decades. Attention Deficit Disorder/ Attention Deficit Hyperactivity Disorder is a syndrome fraught with folklore and misinformation. Prior to more sophisticated and defined diagnostic nomenclature, it was known as minimal brain dysfunction (MBD). In essence and in reality ADD/ADHD is a genetically inherited psychiatric syndrome whose genetic code results in less than normal amounts of dopamine (DA) and/or norepinephrine (NE) in a fairly specific area of the human brain, the prefrontal cortex (PFC). The molecules of DA and NE mediate neuron to neuron, nerve to nerve, communication and function.

Under the leadership of Dr. Stephen Faraone, researchers have identified six to seven "candidate genes" that bring about the cognitive and behavioral presentation seen in people with ADD/ADHD. Five of the genes encode DA function, one encodes for NE availably, and one or two encode for serotonin availability. None of the six are "dominant," all having equal "penetration" or effect, nor do all have to be present or absent for ADD/ADHD to exist or be exhibited in a given person. As you can see, the mathematical combinations or permutations of six to seven genes, present or absent, are infinite. That is specifically why I refer to people with ADD/ADHD as snowflakes, each individual being clearly unique in genetics and clinical presentation, like each individual snowflake, but like each snowflake is a unique individual entity, it is still part of the larger group, snow. It is, therefore, logical statistically and scientifically that I've never seen identical ADD/ADHD patients, despite having seen a number of identical twins, neither can there be a standardized, all-inclusive treatment regimen that fits all ADD/ADHD patients.

The primary symptoms that are the focus of this diagnosis are inattention, hyperactivity, and impulsivity. Historically, boys tend to be diagnosed more frequently and at an earlier age than girls because they tend to generally exhibit the hyperactivity and impulsive behaviors, and, as the saying goes, "the squeaky wheel gets the oil."

Significantly, there has not been any gender prevalence established. Therefore, the syndrome is equally distributed between girls and boys and women and men, with girls and women tending to be under diagnosed since they tend to be of the more inattentive type.

It's hard enough being good parents, but what if, through no fault of their own—they probably got the genes from one of you two anyway—your child cannot pay attention to what you are saying or attempting to demonstrate by example. How can he or she possibly mature properly? The obvious answer is they can't! Therefore, it is most important from a developmental standpoint that there be an early, accurate diagnosis and implementation of a treatment intervention, whether including medication or not.

In real time and in the real world, ADD is simply a shorter than normal ability to pay attention. Unless you've been tested, you don't actually know how long your attention span really is. The average attention span is eighteen to twenty-two minutes. So when does less attention time become problematic? If we go by the standardized test modules like the one developed by Dr. Michael Gordon, the Gordon Diagnostic System, the bubble between reasonable attention and a clear-cut "deficit" is about nine minutes. Some of the children I have referred for testing turned out to have attention spans of a minute or less! Ouch! How can these children possibly learn anything in school or benefit from any and all efforts at parenting?

The need is obvious for early diagnosis and intervention. But, remember they are all snowflakes and distinctly individual. What about the child who can focus for a time period somewhere closer to the nine-minute bubble. In my experience and clinical practice, quite a number of these children can manage quite effectively without any medication; often counseling and educating the parents, plus communication with a teacher about a visual or verbal cueing system, seat assignment, or similar actions are effective enough. However, such interventions will require a lot of work by the parents and the psychiatrist, not to mention a willing, capable, and highly motivated teacher.

When it becomes clear that medication should be considered in the overall treatment plan, what medication will be the most effective for this particular snowflake child or adult?

The answer is more comprehensively discussed in addendum 2.

However, before we charge "where angels fear to tread" in the next chapter, I would like to emphasize that I hope your child will have at least one internal self-face that he or she can fall back on in times of stress and turmoil.

What face? Why is it so important? As you will see, adolescence is a chaotic, unsettling, and distressing time during which your child will experience many challenges and extreme pressures, especially peer pressure.

It will be a time of strange and provocative hairstyles, hair colors, clothing styles, music, language, behavior, alcohol, drugs, and sexual acting out! If your child has a self-face that enhances his or her self-esteem and brings some self-comfort and self-confidence, then his or her resistance to act out will be greatly strengthened. So, if your child feels confident in areas like music, the arts, sports, or other real-time activities such as scouting or church youth groups, they won't feel as lost, overwhelmed, or desperately driven to knuckle under and follow the crowd, that lemming like, is frenetically searching helter-skelter for some meaning, quick fix, or escape from the confusion and despair of the adolescent existence.

Of almost equal magnitude is the carryover of at least one love-tagged adult face to serve as a positive, steadying force as the child enters this time of emotional upheaval and great instability.

Are you ready for the earthquake of adolescence? If you are, then as the famous silver-haired ring announcer hawks, "Let's get ready to rumble!"

5

Sense of Nonsense

Pubescence or adolescence brings the onset of the most challenging and troubling psychological phase in a person's life. One has
to develop, define, and redefine multiple internal faces as well as
the external faces that are continuously presented to the world at
large for the rest of every individual's life. Whoever it was that supposedly stated that the teenage years are the "best years" of your
life, so go out and enjoy them to the fullest, was basically full of you
know what or in a coma, real or emotional, for those years of his or
her own life.

As I see it, there are at least five major developmental hurdles to
clear during adolescence: educational, physical, sexual, separation-
individuation, and facial.

Taking the five challenges in order as noted, we will start with
the faces of education. During latency the child's educational life
is essentially uncomplicated and easy, basically stress-free. As you
transition from primary to middle school, and if you behave within
reasonable social perimeters, you will be seen as a well-behaved
and well-mannered young lady or young man. On the other hand,
if you misbehave, and if multiple interventions by teachers, school
administrators, and parents meet with little to no success, your next
destination is probably the shrink's office!

As the child already has seen and experienced, the educational process in primary or elementary school is essentially "parroting." To somewhat oversimplify, the elementary-level teacher says that "cat" is spelled c-a-t and clearly writes the three letters on the board. She then asks for a show of hands indicating who in the class thinks they can spell cat—the responsive number of hands raised belong mostly to girls—and, guess what, cat shows up on the next spelling quiz. Math is an equally simple educational experience with 2 + 2 = 4. The teacher says it. Students repeat it verbatim. No analytic thinking is necessary nor required for success at this educational level—parrot learning at its very simplistic best.

Life is sweet and simple. Your mother picks out your clothes for the day, makes sure you have a nutritious, well-balanced breakfast, checks to see if your hands and precious little face are clean, slips on and adjusts the Transformers, Fantastic Four, or Hello Kitty back- pack or hands you the commercially endorsed lunch box, and you're good to go. A last-moment hug, kiss on the cheek, and "I love you," and you're out the front door and on your way.

You eagerly get on the "cheese wagon," aka the yellow school bus, for the trip to school. During the bus ride you play your handheld video game device, plug into your iPod, or chat with your friends. When you arrive at school, you go directly to your designated class- room and to your assigned seat with its attached writing area and storage space below. Backpack or lunch box go under your seat, and you're ready to spend the day with wonderful Ms. Smith.

That was elementary school. This is middle school: Wake up, people! If you show up with your Hello Kitty backpack or Teenage Mutant Ninja Turtles lunch box, you will be lucky to get home in one piece or, for that matter, alive! Although this personal style thing is of major importance and will be addressed later in this chapter, let's refocus on the educational process itself.

The bitter truth is that your days of being a parrot are over! No more c-a-t spells cat. But, before we further clarify your un-feather- ing here, remember your comfy desk chair unit, the brightly deco- rated classroom, and the warm and fuzzy Ms. Smith? Forget it! Now you have to change classes. No more one, familiar classroom. No more storing all your belongings securely under your seat. Now, you have been assigned a metal locker! And, it comes with a combina- tion lock! Hopefully, you are assigned the lower locker if you haven't hit your pubescent growth spurt yet, as trying to work a combination lock while on your tiptoes with your arms fully extended may be just too much to ask for or accomplish within the few minutes allowed between class bells.

Oh, those few short minutes to get from one classroom to the next! The challenge is to get from your homeroom, usually your English class, to your math, social studies, geography, earth science, and health/PE classes, all in far-flung areas of the school. No more is friendly Ms. Smith there to encourage, support, and direct you. Instead, you get a map! And, judging by the map, the next classroom is never right next door. Perceptually, judging by the maze of corridors and stairwells, further complicated with the indication that some corridors are actually "one way," your second class appears to be somewhere in the next zip code! Based on this perceived reality there is so little time to get to your second class that stopping by your locker, keeping in mind that you got the upper unit, is definitely out of the question!

If that wasn't enough stress on the new sixth graders, there is always the dark prince, aka the assistant principal, moving stealthily on soft rubber-soled shoes through the halls, constantly patrolling and ready to strike without warning from around a corner or from some other secret hiding place, always smilingly prepared to award a tardy slip and the instruction that you have to report to "the office" at the end of the school day. No wonder the new middle school students are often seen lugging their heavy, bulging, book-laden backpacks the entire school day. They struggle with their heavy burdens from class to class, imagining the tune of a Russian dirge or Mick Jagger wailing "beast of burden" as they trudge along.

The no-parrot system of the middle school educational endeavor begins in earnest a few weeks into the fall semester after subject review has been completed, serving as a bridge between last year's and the current curriculum. This review, despite its good educational intentions, may and often does misleads students into thinking that sixth grade is going to be the proverbial "piece of cake." Usually, the eye-opening reality hits home when Mr. Kowalski, your Mr. Rogers-esque pre-algebra teacher tells you and your classmates that pre-algebra is going to be "so, so much fun." "It'll be like playing a game or solving riddles." In response to these statements you experience an almost uncontrollable urge to stick your index finger as far past your tongue as humanly possible and induce a massive gag reflex! Hell, you never did like solving riddles anyway! No more 2 + 2 = 4. Now you are supposed to solve for "x" and "y"! When you get that concept down pat in a week or two, the class will quickly move on to solving for sign, cosign, and tangent. Oh, to be back in Ms. Smith's class! As your mind is overwhelmed by all this and is fast approaching default mode, your doodling during math class, understanding that you are supposed to be solving for "x," starts to take on an uncanny resemblance to the "x" diagram from your favorite NFL team's playbook, and this endeavor will definitely not result in your scoring a touchdown in pre-algebra or any other class for that matter. Quite to the contrary, your math grade will likely more closely resemble the "D" in "D" "Fence," often seen on signs in the crowd during NFL games.

As if the shock and awe produced by pre-algebra isn't enough of a trauma and potentially quite disorientating, along comes social studies with its focus on government and how the government works. How, may I ask, can we expect a sixth grader to understand the intricate workings of the U.S. Government well enough to attain an A or B in this subject while we have politicians at the state level and in Washington, D.C., who, by their actions and words, have clearly proven that they have absolutely no idea how the U.S. Government really works or is supposed to work! More frightening would be the thought that some of these politicians actually really do know, but they really don't care or give a damn!

Next on the list is Geography. Wow! Are you kidding? Unless your family has had money enough to travel, then the only geography you really know is the backyard and where your favorite store is located in the mall. Although you should care about understanding the land masses of the earth, who cares about identifying all the countries of Africa, their boundaries and names having changed over the years, plus naming their capital cities, while there is little to no chance that you can name all fifty states, their capital cities, and the U.S. territories.

You follow Geography with Earth Science, another beauty of a subject. Here you learn about the raging debate over global warming, your first real taste of politics. Your teacher waxes poetic about the "greenhouse effect" and its impact on our planet. You start to become suspicious that your parents are evil, polluting anti-environmentalists because of the family SUV! You are taught to fear global, environmental Armageddon as the direct effect of increasing greenhouse gases like carbon dioxide and methane.

The future of humanity looks bleak unless something is done! Everyone has to do his or her part. However, you also learn some very interesting scientific facts, like the greatest global source of methane is bovine flatulence, cow farts! So you figure, based on proven scientific evidence, the planet will be much better off without your classmate, Fred, who rather continuously exhibits auditory and olfactory flatulence. As an alternative plan, and clearly more humane than killing Fred, is totally eliminating beans from human consumption worldwide!

Finally, there is Health/PE where you learn the ditty about "this bone is connected to that bone" and the sanitary value of washing your hands after using the toilet. Hopefully, washing your hands isn't a new event in your life by the time you get to middle school, especially after going to the bathroom!

Probably more stressful than the learning part of Health is the dressing-out part of PE. If you haven't already become aware of and are extremely self-conscious of your body's changing shape and size, or lack thereof, then it will become a real issue when you are required to strip off your clothes and change into your gym uniform in front of all your peers, or possibly even more stressful, under the watchful, voyeuristic gaze of your PE teacher. You believe, or for sure heard it rumored, that he's a certified pervert!

So, there it is, the first of the five developmental hurdles of adolescence, and frighteningly there are only four more to come. So many traumatizing potholes, accidents, and IEDs specific to this stretch of life's highway are lurking on the road ahead. An unfamiliar, and as the kids would say "humongous," school with one-way halls, the upper-tier padlocked locker, unforgiving upperclassmen, the Draculian assistant principal, parrot learning replaced with the introduction of subjects that require understanding and conceptualization, different teachers conspiring to assign massive homework so as to ruin any fun plans for after school or on the weekends and the switch from the Satisfactory/Unsatisfactory grading system to the A to E or F system all significantly impact and sculpt the child's educational face.

How will teachers and others see your child? What face will they see? How will your child see themselves in terms of their belief in education's value and how much is enough education, how far to ultimately go?

Related to all this, here are some Tsaoism observations and thoughts that might be helpful to you and, more importantly, to your child. Hopefully, after digesting what you've read so far, you have some understanding, or the material as presented has triggered some memory, about how overwhelming the physical plant of your child's new middle school can truly be. We have all experienced new places as generally vast, unfamiliar, and somewhat overwhelming, daunting. We anxiously doubt whether we will ever be able to navigate to where we need to go. With time, experience, and repetition we come to realize that our anxieties were totally and completely unfounded. If adults experience this, for example when we change jobs or move to a new neighborhood or city, consider how much more stressful this experience must be for your child whose experience of change up to this point in life has been so much more limited. They have no experience to draw upon.

With that being said, many enlightened school systems around the country actually offer the opportunity to tour your child's new middle school before the fall semester begins. Take advantage of this offer. If your school system doesn't offer such an opportunity formally, then contact the administration of your child's new school and ask if you can independently tour with your child. Explore, as much as possible, the entire building. Show your daughter or son the different classrooms. Demonstrate that you can get from one classroom to another in a reasonable amount of time without stressing out. Actually time it. You can even make some sort of game out of the experience. Include those metal lockers on your itinerary, commenting how nice it will be to have a secure place for your child's belongings. Stay positive. Extol a can-do attitude.

Should there be some teachers around, stop and introduce yourself and your child. Here's a hint: Teachers genuinely like the idea that a student has an involved, education-invested parent. This effort might even garner some "brownie points" for your child in the upcoming school year, and that can't be a bad thing. It's paramount to understand that a child's attitude and commitment to education hinge not only upon your words, but even more so upon your actions. So, make the effort here. It can pay big dividends in the future for you and your child.

My next observation and recommendation to parents is to make every effort to be aware of pre-teen and early teen fashion in your particular community. Be assured that your child is acutely aware and, if not already so, will soon become so. When shopping for back-to-school clothes, allow your child to make some choices, even if the choices aren't necessarily to your liking. After all, it's the child who has to wear the different items of clothing to school. Donate the Spider-Man, Batman, Barbie, Hello Kitty, and other such items of clothing to Goodwill or a similar agency. This effort will assist your child's social and peer acceptance in the new school, this acceptance being a very important thing to your child's overall adjustment to the middle school experience. A small tax deduction for the donated clothes doesn't hurt either.

Further thoughts about this time include the importance of the parents, together or separate, understanding the shift in the grading system. Prior to middle school the grading system is designed to document whether or not a particular student is progressing as expected. S indicates "satisfactory" progress; U indicates that there is a potential or real problem. The A, B, C system marks the change from rote learning (parroting) to the phasing in of abstract and analytic thinking to the educational process, like solving for "x" and "y."

Although your child may be quite bright or even of superior intelligence, not all children develop abstract or analytic capability at the same chronologic age. This may particularly affect math performance. Additionally, understand that your child has no previous experience nor has he or she developed any coping skills in how to deal with six different teachers, their six different personalities, their six different teaching styles, and their six different expectations. Can you imagine having six different bosses at work, all with essentially equal authority? Nightmare, huh? Make an investment of extra time and involvement in the early weeks of the school year to help your child get organized. Ask how they are getting along

with their different teachers. Don't accept nondescript, generic answers.

Sadly, I am unaware of any Internet sites that rate middle school
teachers in the way that such sites rate college professors. Your extra involvement and support at this particular transition time can
pay big emotional and academic dividends in the future.

With all this transition work and its inherent stress and confusion, be prepared for your angelic genius to bring home his or her
first less than satisfactory grade! Be aware of and guard against the
parental knee-jerk reaction to punish the child for this under-par
grade, potentially inaccurately assuming a lack of effort, irrespon-
sibility, or too much self-indulgence on the child's part. It is exactly
this knee-jerk reaction that motivates kids to hide their progress
reports showing lack of progress, or their report cards documenting
less than acceptable grades. They're not stupid! They have places to
go, people to see, and things to do, and they don't want a progress
report or report card putting a crimp in their plans.

Too often parents take away television time, computer time, or
phone time. Play time and all contact with friends are severely restricted or eliminated. All these measures may ultimately be necessary, but slow down and consider that there are multiple potential
reasons for your child's poor grade(s) beyond a wish to shine you
off! Don't turn your child's education into one of the major battlegrounds of adolescence! Trust me, in this situation nobody really
wins.

For example, if your child has not been a behavior problem in
elementary school, and previously made satisfactory progress and
grades, then why is there a problem now? I've always wondered why
so often there is such a negative, punitive parental response. It's not
like there would be whispers at church or diverted gazes at the mall
indicating public censure, or that one morning you, as the parent,
will awaken to find a bumper sticker attached to your vehicle stating that you are the "embarrassed" parent of a failing middle school
student! Parents act as though their child has done all this to embarrass them personally. On the other hand, probably closer to the
truth is that the child is actually struggling with adjusting to a new
and developmentally challenging subject like pre-algebra.

Two realities may be at work here. First, the class itself may be too advanced for your child. Second, it could be genetics. Were you a "math wiz" when you were your child's age? Did punishment by your parents improve your grades or effort? My recommendation here is to seek the advice and guidance of your child's math teacher. Transferring to a less advanced or accelerated class might be the ticket to success. Your child will catch up eventually and will appreciate your understanding and help. So avoid the knee-jerk reaction. Try to understand and don't punish as a "first" option.

More advice to parents and kids is to hit the ground running at the start of middle school and every grade thereafter. The saying, "You never get a second chance to make a first impression," once again truly applies here. I always exhort my patients to be on time, be polite, be positive, pay attention in class or at least pretend to, do all your homework and turn it in, and stop whining about summer vacation being over! Do all this for the first six weeks because at the end of that time period the teachers will have to produce a progress report on each and every student in their classes.

Your child wants to achieve two of three options at this juncture. First, and of course best, is a positive progress report, the teacher's impression and perception of your child being that it is a "pleasure" to have them in the classroom. The second, and almost as good a report, is a vague or neutral progress report, indicating that the student left no impression one way or the other in her teacher's mind. The third and unwanted possibility is the "negative" progress report identifying the student as a clear-cut problem. This negative report then triggers the requirement for a follow-up progress report, whereas the first two options don't. Let me repeat, the first two progress report options don't!

First of all, teachers, like all the rest of us, don't like extra work without extra pay, which a negative progress report will require of them. The potential second negative report after the first nine weeks will solidify in the teacher's mind a negative perception of your child from that point in time forward. Remember the power of thought insertion? The negative report and the resultant teacher's negative perception of the particular student usually means that the teacher probably will never cut that particular student any slack for the rest of the school year, whereas more leniency is granted to the students with the positive or neutral progress reports. It's really just a matter of common sense.

For example, if the student is borderline passing at the end of the semester, the teacher is more likely than not to fail the negative-report student. For students with positive or neutral progress reports, they are more likely to be passed. So, hit the ground running for the first six weeks! Please! If you don't, then consider that if the first six weeks don't go well, the remaining thirty weeks—that's right, the remaining "thirty" long weeks of the school year—can become a living hell for the student and their parents!

A final thought about education before we move on: Having gotten past the first nine weeks of senior year, a commonly experienced dilemma occurs for parents: "college applications."

Assuming that your child has made decent enough grades and has scored high enough on the SATs, it's time to complete college applications and get them turned in on time. That's the problem, getting them "turned in on time." As the deadline approaches, meaning that if your teenager's application isn't completed and received by the chosen institution of higher education, your kid is "dead" in relation to attending that particular college. This situation wouldn't be so bad or disturbing if only one or two applications were incomplete. But the usual situation is that none of them is done and the clock is literally ticking! The "dead" line is fast approaching. Tension over this is rising with each tick of the clock and the passing of each day.

What's a parent supposed to do if and when this situation rears its ugly head? Encourage? Cajole? Threaten? Restrict? Punish? Or should you choose none of the above? Understand that college applications, unless your youngster is only applying to the local community college and intends to live at home for the next two years, documents for your teenager that despite all their complaining, rebellious behavior, and statements that they just can't wait to move the hell out and live on their own, underneath it all they "really are" going to have to leave home. I mean, for real, they're going to have to leave home! Your teenager, soon to be an adult, is going to leave their nice comfy room and home base, a community that they know like the palm of their hand, and their close circle of friends, among other things. They have so many reasons, real and psychological, working against the completion of those applications. Therefore, the conscious or unconscious way not to have to face leaving home is obviously not to complete the applications!

Parents often react by saying, "Well, it's their future. So, if they don't get them done, then, 'Oh well'"! Uh . . . think about this for a second. You've worked and suffered through seventeen to nineteen years, hoping that your child will move out and move on. Right? Do you really want your daughter or son to be under your feet for another two to four years? I thought not! Thus, the advice that I give these worried and anxious parents is to do the applications for their children. That's right! After working with thousands of patients and their families, I can tell you that this strategy really works. Trust me! It works because your teen may not be able to complete the applications for the reasons I've already clarified. Therefore, mom and dad do those applications for loving and "selfish" reasons.

Second, it's an unknown and totally new experience for them, not unlike that which occurred when the child was dropped off for the first time at daycare. Therefore, this going away to college thing, compared to transferring from elementary to middle school and eventually to high school, can be and often is psychologically overwhelming. This time they'll have to really leave home, and "homesickness" is a frequently experienced malady for freshmen who go away to college, sometimes emotionally debilitating enough that they eventually have to withdraw from their freshman classes and move back home.

Third, getting the applications in on time or even early may result in your child being accepted at one of his or her or your top choices. Early application is also associated with the availability of potential grant or scholarship monies. Do it! You'll thank me someday as thousands of parents have done so already.

Clearly, college is just one of the many doors of opportunity that will open for your child when they have their high school diploma in hand. Whereas, for those without a high school diploma the trapdoor to potential lifelong problems related to their future success and quality of life will open up right underneath their very feet, and down they'll go!

The second challenge of adolescence is physical. Coming out of elementary school, children, with few exceptions, are all essentially munchkin-like in size. Generally speaking, just prior to or during sixth grade, growth hormone production starts to ramp up and the children, particularly the boys, will experience "growth spurts." Girls and boys, like weeds in the summer, can sprout up almost in front of your very eyes. Growing one to three inches during the summer months alone is not unusual. This reality is well documented, if not by the actual measurement by the pediatrician, then by the need to alter pant legs as they are suddenly inches too short and purchase new shoes, as the current footwear is clearly too small.

During this time of rapid growth, a medical-neurological phenomenon will also become quite noticeable. The root of the observed behavior is grounded in the scientific fact that bone, muscle, and tendon can grow or lengthen much more rapidly than nerves. This causes behavior to emerge that is not unlike why babies can't walk right away, even though they have feet.

Remember that babies basically cannot walk early on because their wiring, neurons, and nerves are not insulated, or myelinated. Similar but not exactly identical, here the rapid extension of muscle, tendon, and bone is not temporally matched by the lengthening of the associated neurons/nerves, resulting in the child's proprioceptive neurons needing some time to catch up. Since proprioception facilitates our knowing where our hands and feet are in relationship to the rest of our body without actually looking at them, lack of this function is exhibited as clumsiness. Think of it this way: When we walk, as a general rule, we don't look down to watch where our feet are going every step of the way. Ben Crenshaw, one of the historically great putters on the PGA tour, said that if you're not sure which way a putt turns or breaks, or whether it's very slightly uphill or downhill, then walk near the intended line and your feet will give you the answer. Now that's taking full advantage of your proprioceptive abilities! Maybe "Gentle Ben," as he was known during his regular tour-playing days, had better proprioceptive abilities in his feet than the rest of us hackers.

This explains the observed behavior of people who have lost their proprioceptive function due to age, illness, or intoxication. The "slapping gait" is one of the diagnostic signs of people who have developed a peripheral neuropathy, nerve damage in their arms and/or legs, the result of years of alcohol abuse or some other metabolic or neurologic disease.

This dysfunction has been readily observable for years in my hometown of Virginia Beach, Virginia. For decades there has been a nightclub near the oceanfront favored by the young locals. The club itself occupies the second story of the building, and entrance and egress is provided by a long, fairly wide, somewhat steep, red-carpeted staircase with a landing area at the halfway point. There are handrails on both sides, but most impressive is the polished brass railing that extends top to bottom dissecting the stairwell in equal halves. Since I was friends with one of the owners of the club then, and in order to keep up with the most current goings-on with many of my patients, I would now and then quietly and as unobtrusively as possible visit and observe the human menagerie in action. What I witnessed was the progressive loss of proprioception! Early in the evening, young people would quickly go up and down the stairs without the slightest compunction to use the brass rail, nor ever looking down at their feet, even though there were many young ladies wearing ridiculously high heels. But, as the evening wore on and alcohol consumption progressed, the shiny brass rail gained a lot of handprints and smudges, becoming a necessity with many people holding on and carefully watching each and every one of their steps, ascending or most particularly descending. Despite this observed behavioral change late in the evening, there were still many stumbles and falls as the staff of Peabody's would honestly attest. The young patrons had clearly lost their proprioception and couldn't be sure where their feet were located in relationship to the red carpet!

Ah! Now we have a real understanding of the reason behind the police and their "field sobriety test" before they insist on the use of a breathalyzer. They want to determine if the person in question knows where his feet actually are! Therefore, my advice is that if you have to look down at your feet to leave a restaurant or club, call a cab. You've had way too much to drink! If you observe that your date or the designated driver in the group is looking down at his or her feet while they're trying to walk out, insist on the keys!

Accordingly, children exhibit similar behavior during and immediately following growth spurts, sort of acting like they've had too much to drink. They will become like the proverbial bull in a china shop. This is a time of many, many bumps and bruises and not infrequently even broken bones. The kids bruise and break not only themselves, but other people and objects around them. Please understand that they basically cannot help it. They are not doing it on purpose to make you mad or to intentionally hurt you or destroy your personal property. Being verbally critical or derogatory just isn't very helpful. Your child is having more than enough trouble in this phase of development trying to establish some level of self-confidence, an acceptable self-face, and physical self-competence. So, try to be understanding and supportive. Take the time to explain to your pre-teen or early teenager during this time of clumsiness that what is happening to their body, physically and neurologically, is normal. Share with him or her that you yourself or an older sibling went through the same or similar experience, and that you or big sister or brother turned out okay. Hopefully, that's true! In any case, reassure your child that it will all turn out fine, given the tincture of time. Do this and you can reduce this pothole in the road of life to the smallest possible emotional bump, leaving no significant damage to the undercarriage of your child's psyche.

Challenge number three of adolescence is sexual. Of course, this challenge is concomitantly and intricately tied to the physical growth vertically, but growth in this phase is not just up. The physical and psychological development here is initiated by the onset of and the influence of sex hormones.

During the previous developmental phase, girls and boys are, for all intents and purposes, unisex. Girls are happy and content to socialize and play only with other little girls. As far as the boys are concerned, the feeling is definitely mutual—although observed human behavior confirms that they have not and probably never will give up the Electra or Oedipus complexes totally. Accordingly, throughout adolescence girls still tend to exhibit quite a bit of "daddy's little girl" behavior. This may not be such a bad thing; as a result of this girls feel that no male can come close to being as lovable or looked up to as their own father. This can decrease and/or delay the onset of the boy-crazy developmental phenomenon. As girls perceive their daddy as wonderful, they will see boys as yucky, disgusting, dirty, rough, and despicable. On the other side of the fence, boys, also never totally giving up Oedipus, see their mothers as essentially perfect and worthy of love, resulting in the perception that most girls are annoying and have little to no real intrinsic value.

As we will see later on, the major psychological goal of adolescence, separation-individuation, is essential, albeit a loss for mom and dad, so that the child can grow up emotionally and have the chance to participate in a noncompetitive, committed, loving adult relationship, a goal universally sought after, but seldom attained.

Here's an observation for adults and couples related to marriage. First, take a close look at the relationship that existed, and to some degree may still exist, with the parent of the opposite sex, and the parental relationship overall.

Guys, were you the apple of your mother's eye, her superstar, her "little man," supported and loved without condition or reservation? Did mom devotedly do everything for you that she possibly could and far beyond? Did she cater to your every whim or need, either expressed or intuitively understood? Did mom easily excuse and forgive your faults, mistakes, and transgressions? If so, then here is the real question: Is it really fair or realistic to expect this from your girlfriend or wife? Ya think? If you haven't figured this out by now, you're already in or soon will be in a world of hurt. Dude, your girlfriend, fiancée, or wife is not your mother! So get used to it and adjust to this reality! Give it up and grow up!

The problem is that men generally portray themselves as the strong and silent type; that is our externalized persona for all the world to see. However, in many ways underneath that tough exterior we're just a bunch of mommy's boys and can get our feelings hurt rather easily. Consider that where your mommy nurtured, loved, and praised you based on her unconditional love, and when you stumbled and scraped your knee, actually or figuratively, she was the first one to tell you "it's okay," that she loved you as she propped you up for the next challenge of life. On the other side of the coin, your wife or significant other is the first, but probably not the last, woman to chime in and point out after one of your stumbles that you're "stupid"!

Men sometimes openly express, but much more frequently they cover up their hurt feelings, thinking to themselves, "My mommy would never have talked to me like that!"

If you men—and I should note grossly unrealistically—have the expectation that a relationship or marriage to a woman should be like the relationship you had with your mother, then maybe you should do what Oedipus did! I have worked with many an exasperated wife who wished that her husband would do just that, leave and go back to his "mommy"! Men, think about what am I presenting to you here in the hope that you may consider all this and possibly effect some positive change in yourself, your expectations, and ultimately your relationship with that significant woman in your life.

Before you get too smug, ladies, consider the following about your part and responsibility in all of this. On some level are you still expecting to be treated like "daddy's little princess"? Understand that your expectations of your boyfriend, fiancé, or husband may be equally too lofty and unrealistic. After all, just as you are not his mommy, he is equally not your daddy! Although there by nature must be some of this in all marriages, the question is how much does this emotional baggage, if you will, impede the growth of or actually damage the current relationship.

The part about falling in love, courting, getting married, and the fantasy honeymoon is easy. It's the "and they lived happily ever after" part I've pointed out before that is the real challenge! This is when the unresolved Oedipus/Electra previously experienced family relational conflicts and related expectations will lead to frustration, anger, hurt feelings, dysfunction, and divorce. As I have explained many times to people in my therapeutic work, anger is in essence the perception or belief that one is not getting what he or she deserves, realistic or unrealistic. In effect, if we believe we are getting what we deserve out of life, then we're a bunch of happy campers. As Karl Marx was reported to have said, "Religion is the opiate of the people." Even though as a Communist he was an atheist despite his previous religious belief, he was pleased that the peasants and other common folk had religion, so that they would truly thank God for their bowl of porridge and small piece of bread. In this state of mind, being thankful for what little they had, they were less likely to be angry and, as a result, less likely to rise up and revolt against the oppressive Communist regime.

Refocusing on marriage, take an honest look at yourself in the mirror of reality. Look carefully and try to see how your relationship with your mom or dad, with all its resolved and unresolved issues, may still be emotionally and behaviorally impacting you and your current relationship or future relationships or marriage. But I'll discuss much more about this later in addendum 1.

Back to the kids. With the uptick of female sexual hormones, an event of great magnitude in a girl's life literally bursts upon the scene: menstruation, a word that appears to be absolutely forbidden and taboo in American society. Based on my clinical experience it is such a forbidden word that for the most part it is never discussed or mentioned prior to the onset of the event itself. Whereas women in other societies like Europe and the Pacific Rim openly discuss and prepare their daughters for the "estrous cycle," American mothers generally don't. This is probably related in some way to America's general sexual oppressiveness, possibly dating back to the Puritanical origins of our society.

Mothers generally approach the subject with the "leave it to the school system" method, "read this pamphlet or book" method, or the frank denial method, holding on to the hope that if we don't talk about it, then maybe it will just go away and won't ever actually happen. Great! This last method leaves the girl completely and totally unprepared for her first menstrual period!

I have worked with many a young woman, the recipients of the denial method, who share with me how upsetting and confusing it was with their first menstruation. With some bitterness, related to their ignorance of the biologic facts, they have reported that they initially believed they had somehow injured themselves "down there" or had a bladder infection or something else seriously wrong with them physically. Very seldom, actually closer to never, have I heard that an American mother joyfully shared with her premenstrual daughter anything about the impending "wonderful event" that will herald her entrance into womanhood and the amazing "blessing" of being able to then bear children. The story I'm generally told is the extreme opposite of this stated position. Much, much more commonly the girls hear, "You've been real moody lately" or "You've been really bitchy" or "You're PMSing big time!" or "The curse is about to happen" or "You show all the signs" or "You look bloated" or "Do you have a migraine? Sure you do! That's when my headaches started too"! Wow! What a positive female attitude and experience for the adolescent girl. Just kidding of course, but consider the negative emotional fallout from this approach to menstruation. Never forget the power of thought insertion, its implementation consciously or unconsciously, and its impact good or bad on the human mind—in this case the mind of the daughter in question.

To further compound this negative emotional experience, menstruation inevitably leads to the instruction of how to use "sanitary napkins," implying that somehow menstruation is "infected" or "dirty." And here I thought that a sanitary napkin was what restaurants put out with the rest of the table setting! The alternative feminine hygiene product is a tampon, given to the young lady with an instruction like, "Just stick this thing up there and try not to make a mess of it." More commonly, girls are just given this white paper-wrapped, cigar-shaped object without any instruction whatsoever!

Further confirmation of our puritanical roots, with some Roman Catholic flavor thrown into the mix for good measure, was documented when my then three-year-old granddaughter fell awkwardly and hurt herself during playtime while attending a Catholic preschool. She ran up to and complained to one of the nuns that she had hurt her "vagina." Hearing the word vagina, all the other little children went into a behavioral tizzy accompanied by a chorus of "Oh . . . what you said!"

Psychiatrically, it seems to me that we are obligated to change this long-established socio-cultural behavioral pattern. We really need to de-stigmatize normal physical sexual development. Menstruation shouldn't be a "dirty" word. A vagina is a vagina; a penis, a penis. As a society we shouldn't attach so much mystery and taboo to our human sexuality.

As the father of psychoanalytic symbolism allegedly noted during a lecture while holding up a cigar for all to see, "Gentlemen, this may be a phallic symbol, but it's nonetheless just a cigar." No kidding! I think, if Freud were around today, he might agree with me: Despite all of the emotionality attached to it, just as a cigar is just a cigar, sex is just sex! If we as a society could reach more of an "it is what it is" attitude about sex and sexuality, there would be a lot fewer people with "hang-ups," the real potentially negative fallout from this emotionally charged area of human physical and psychological development.

This hormonal surge also miraculously alters the little girl's view of boys. Whereas boys were previously the objects of disdain and disgust, they almost overnight become "so, so cute." This perception usually progresses to the emotional malady that's called being "boy crazy," a behavior that is generally universally exhibited by preadolescent and early adolescent girls.

For the boys, the onset and increased testicular production of hormones noticeably leads to masculinization of the vocal cords, ending any potential career in the boys' choir. But, clearly of more importance and impact for guys, the increased testosterone levels initiate the development of the male anatomical pattern of hair distribution. Although this hair growth occurs in all hair distribution pattern areas of the young man's anatomy, facial hair is the real deal as it is the outward and visible sign of developing masculinity.

At some juncture during this developmental time, the young man will ask his parents to purchase a razor for him. Despite the reality that most of what he wants to shave would more closely meet the criteria for peach fuzz, my advice would be to go ahead and spend the money on the multi-bladed, Teflon-enhanced, latest killer razor product!

What your son will be going through or is now going through reminds me of that time in my life. I can still clearly see the first guy in my school who had to shave, and I emphasize "had to." Joe had a dark, rough five o'clock shadow by the end of the school day, and it wasn't even five o'clock yet! I went to an all boys' Catholic high school, and all the rest of the guys felt envious and at least a little inferior to Joe, knowing that his hirsutism documented that he was a real sexual animal. Joe was the man!

Due to our overall ignorance and naivete at that age, how were we to know or understand that Joe's beard was more related to him being of Italian decent, and nothing more than that. At a class reunion years later Joe's fullness of beard was contrarily and equally matched by his baldness of head. I guess justice is rendered now and then after all! In any case, being of Asian extraction, and as a result of this, having a relatively hairless body, I was one of the last of my friends to shave. I still remember my sense of fulfillment the day I nicked myself while shaving so that I had to apply that whitish stuff to the nick to stop the small amount of bleeding. I went to school that day with the treated nick clearly visible on my cheek for all too see. Ah! I made it into the men's club!

This rite of passage for boys is equally matched emotionally and developmentally in a not dissimilar experience for young women. It has a great impact on their self-perceived femininity and self-esteem.

With rising levels of estrogen, the formerly unisex-shaped little girl starts to develop curves. As facial hair was clearly visible for all to see and is the external sign of masculinity, the increase of breast size is the external sign of developing femininity. All the girls become acutely aware of who in their peer group first had to, and I once again emphasize "had to," wear a training bra. Now, this presents a dilemma for parents similar to whether to buy the super killer razor for their son. Should you, driven by your daughter's insistent requests, purchase that training bra? Like the peach fuzz scenario, it doesn't seem to make much sense. I mean, what is the training brassiere supposed to do? What is it supposed to train your daughter's small developing breasts to do? Sit up? Roll over? Play dead? Once again, all kidding aside, and disregarding financial practicality, please spend the money! It is an important rite of passage for your daughter and has great impact on her self-image, self-face, perceived femininity, and self-esteem. We have already discussed the psychological mechanism underlying the emotional value of breasts in a previous chapter.

As razors and training bras let the world know that your sons and daughters are developing a sexual identity, and as "the curse" of menstruation is the secret, unspoken event documenting womanhood, what is the secret unspoken event for the boys?

As we have seen at this stage of development, girls make a 180 degree turnaround in their feelings about and perception of the attractiveness of boys, similarly boys are experiencing a total turnaround in how they view and feel about girls.

Increasing testosterone serum boosts the intensity of interest in girls exponentially. So where previously girls were viewed as annoying and basically useless, they start to become "so, so hot!" The secret event for men usually begins with a dream, a very stimulating, exciting, and climatic dream, so to speak. This "wet dream" is the beginning of the man's near lifelong search for orgasmic "relief" and fulfillment. Prior to the testosterone surge, a boy views his penis as useful as a penis allows him to stand up and urinate without pee dripping or running down one or both of his legs. Now he discovers that his penis has another really amazing pleasurable purpose. The young man has now discovered that "Mr. Happy" works! The male quest "Cher Cher la Femme" for the "fantasy" woman, or sometimes any woman, begins in earnest! This drive or urge is so great that many published studies exist documenting that men, particularly young sexually maturing men, think about sex basically all the time. No kidding! Really?

At this point, when I'm lecturing on human sexual behavior, I have often referenced Charles Darwin and his famous work The Origin of Species, which was published in 1859. This publication explained the theory behind the survival of species and the process of "natural selection." The brilliance of Darwin's thinking and many of his original theories is still held in high esteem by the scientific community to this very day. It is his theories that predict the behaviors of all species, from microorganisms to Homo sapiens. Despite all the psychological theories and schools of thought, at the core of it all, underneath the veneer of education, culture, and religion, humans basically behave according to Darwin's principles whether or not we like or accept this premise as accurate.

I prefer to use rabbits as the species in my analogy explaining Darwin's theories of evolution as related to human behavior. Why bunny rabbits? Well, these soft, cuddly, non-aggressive if not actually quite passive mammals are a great survival story. Besides, I'm writing this book, so why not my choice?

The bunny story starts with the birth of the new generation of baby bunnies into the "Bunny Nation." After weaning, the baby bunnies hop around and eat clover and other greens, and like little children, unless closely physically examined by a veterinarian, you can't tell the doe bunnies from the buck bunnies, all appearing unisex. All is peaceful. As time passes and the bunnies mature, they enter the juvenile stage, equivalent to pre to early adolescence in human beings. At this point, the buck bunnies start to play fight as do the juvenile tigers, cheetahs, and wildebeests. Similarly, boys start to get into competitive sports and other activities that focus their thoughts and activities on strength and masculinity, the human equivalent of play fighting seen in other juvenile mammals. All the young male mammals, including humans, are preparing for the big day.

Finally, when the buck bunnies reach maturity, they engage in a major scrum or battle, during which the fur literally flies. They squeal, attack, thump, and bite each other in earnest. Some of the male rabbits may even die by the end of the day. By now, the boys have reached the same level in sports and often make statements to the effect, "We crushed 'em," "We humiliated 'em," 'We killed them," "We murdered them!"

At the end of the great battle when the dust has settled, one winner will emerge, the "alpha male buck bunny" and, as Bob Barker, the famous game-show host, used to ask, "Johnny, what does he win?" He wins the right to copulate with, have sex with, the most attractive doe bunny! After that comes the next most attractive doe bunny and so on and so on until he is totally exhausted or satiated. Then it is the runner-up buck bunny's turn to choose the partner of his choice from the remaining doe bunnies and so on down the line. Obviously, and sadly, the last buck bunny in line doesn't have much to pick from, if any doe bunnies are even left!

Now, according to Darwin, this is exactly how it's supposed to happen. The alpha male bunny got to be the winner because he was the most adaptable, strong, fast, intelligent, and vicious—all traits, that if passed on to the next generation of baby rabbits, will ensure the survival and success of the Bunny Nation over time.

The story is essentially the same for Homo sapiens, us! All that simulated fighting and competition on the athletic fields are just practice for establishing who in actuality really is Numero Uno, #1. Could it be that Darwin explained through the understanding of his theories why basically no one remembers or cares about who finished second?

The essential difference that separates us from the other members of the mammalian kingdom is that the survival trait that trumps all the others in primacy for human beings is intelligence. To wit, Homo erectus, standing men, and all predecessors to modern man, Homo sapiens, were generally physically stronger and had physical characteristics like hairier, bigger, more muscular bodies, and larger jaws that made them more adapted to cope with the geography, weather, and predators of that geologic time. Archeological findings support that, in fact, erectus and sapiens coexisted for thousands of years on planet Earth. So, if Darwin was right, how did the smaller, generally weaker, and somewhat hairless beings drive their bigger, hairier relatives into extinction? A bigger brain that correlates to greater intelligence is the logical and obvious scientific answer.

Archeology and nueroanatomical principles have established that it takes a minimum amount or mass of cerebral "grey matter" in order to have language. Based on brain cavity size, Homo sapiens had more than this minimum critical mass, and the others human-oids like Homo erectus did not. It follows, metaphorically speak-ing, that when the smaller Homo sapiens were approaching and a confrontation was inevitable, Homo erectus, being handicapped with little or no ability to communicate by language, was left with jumping up and down, finger pointing, fist shaking, chest thump-ing, and other threatening gestures accompanied by a cornucopia of grunts, growls, and screams. This particular behavior is still seen in modern primates whenever they feel threatened. On the other side, Homo sapiens, although equipped with relatively the same primi-tive Stone Age weapons, possessed the ultimate weapon: language, the ability in real-time battle conditions to communicate. While the big hairy guys were jumping up and down and vocalizing threaten-ing sounds, the smaller relatively hairless guys talked to each other and communicated strategies like some of us will confront the big guys head-on and distract them while the rest of us circle around to the side or behind, and when we command the high ground, on verbal signal or command, we'll hit them with rocks from all direc-tions. Clear proof that intelligence and language truly "rules" is that we're here and they're reduced to only bones of archeological inter-est.

The power of intelligence has held serve over the centuries, as proven historically by the rise and fall of civilizations and nations. The "alpha" nations had to have the brain size to conceptualize and technologically produce the most powerful and deadly weapons during each of their times to reign.

Not so long ago, the USSR and the USA were in a tight competi-tion to see who could produce the most frightening and destructive weapons. In fact, as far as we know, much of that information is still "classified." What we do know is that at some point in time both sides had the ability to destroy the world, nuclear Armageddon. The "end of the world" scenario wasn't just political hype, posturing, or fiction writing during the Cold War era. It was a clear and present danger and a real possibility.

With the passage of that troubled time, and with the emergence of the United States as the clearly dominant "alpha" power, the world community at large has taken a few small steps back from the brink of nuclear extinction. Without being able to hold nuclear destruction over each other's heads, our world leaders appear to have taken a page from Homo erectus, in terms of reverting back to jumping up and down, beating their chests, and making verbally threatening sounds! I only hope it stays that way for the sake of the world's current and future population. However, I am concerned that more and more countries are developing or have developed nuclear capability and are pushing us once again toward a doomsday scenario.

All this applies to the microcosm of adolescence. It's about a big brain and the value of education. An uneducated big brain is clearly a wasted advantage. Based on all this information, for civilizations and individuals, clearly the ultimate selector is brain power. We can talk about professional athletes, their special physical talents, their inflated salaries, and how they are the supposedly "alpha" males; however, the real alpha male buck bunnies of our society are the team owners. There is a Big Ten school that over the years has been better known for its academics than athletics. There is reported to be a sign over the entrance to the visiting football team's locker room stating, "You may beat us today, but you will work for us tomorrow." Once again, despite the fame and fortune of Tiger, A-Rod, Kobe, and other superstar athletes, do they really wield more power and influence than Bill Gates, Warren Buffett, Ted Turner, or the Waltons?

As sexuality grows in influence and sexual differentiation progresses, the girls and the boys appear, at least on the surface, to make some illogical and upsetting choices.

An oft-asked question by parents is to challenge me to explain why their daughter is constantly attracted to such "losers." The answer to this question is multifaceted, but really quite understandable and predictable.

First of all, from a sexual and biological drive point of reference, the more hormonally sexually aware and feminine a girl is or becomes, the more attracted she is to guys with the most testosterone! And who are the guys with the most testosterone in high school? You've got it. It's the "bad boys"! The rule breakers and risk takers are so, so interesting and irresistible, and their open disdain for parental or societal rules makes them so, so sexy! The guys who mock and denigrate the geeks and nerds, who consistently strive for good grades and—can you believe this?—actually do their homework, are so hot! Their use of the "F" word as a noun, adverb, or verb and their long hair, Mohawk, or dreadlocks makes the bad boys almost impossible for your daughters to resist. Even after long and at times emotionally trying and heated debates, after which you get your daughter to see "the truth" about her chosen bad boy, you still can't win. Accepting all the negatives about her boyfriend to be true, your daughter's comeback, in effect, will be, "I'll help him change his evil ways." Oh boy! What are you going to do now? What should you have done in the first place?

What I haven't clarified up until this point, but have alluded to previously, is that beyond or in addition to the hormonal, there is the normal, healthy separation-individuation process running simultaneously. Parents should encourage independent thinking and function. Without emotional growth in this sphere of development, your child may never be able to make the leap to independent, functional adulthood.

The struggle for psychological independence can impact almost all aspects of the adolescent's life. Your child needs to rebel! Let me say that again. Your child needs to rebel! It's psychologically and developmentally healthy and normal. The question is in what aspect or area of life should he or she be allowed, even encouraged, to rebel?

The Tsaoism here is, "Parents, you pick the battleground." You pick the battle and fight furiously over that one, something you secretly don't really care about. I mean it! Don't fight over school, religion, morals, work ethic, alcohol and drugs, or significant others. You are fully within your rights to disagree with me, but if you do disagree, then it just makes more work for me and my therapist colleagues. Once again more job security for shrinks!

Accepting my advice as worthwhile, let's look at your daughters
and the "bad boys" more closely. There are three powerful forces
working here. First of all, we have just looked at and now understand that teens need to separate and individuate, rebel. Therefore,
it follows that if you would prefer and actually push your daughter
to associate with the "nice boys," she is going to on some degree feel
compelled to choose the exact opposite. We have already discussed
the hormonal surge, the concept that the more estrogen, the greater
the attraction to the perceived highest testosterone guys as the second driving force.

The third factor is Electra. Prior to this developmental time we
have documented that girls have an over-determined love, attraction, and closeness to their daddies. I can't count the number of
times the divorced, custodial mothers cannot understand why their
daughters still hang on and hope that "my daddy" will come through
even just once, when their no-good, deadbeat, blankity-blank father
never has delivered emotionally for the child in the past, much less
kept up with the child support payments! I tell these mothers not
to worry as this behavior pattern will disappear naturally during
adolescence.

During childhood and latency, it is normal behavior for a little
girl to give lots of hugs and kisses to her daddy. The sharing of time,
experiences, and physical closeness are all the rage. With the onset
of menstruation and a developing sense of her own sexuality, the
taboo of incest, either conscious or subliminal, drives the teenage
girl to distance herself from her father. Where desirable in previous developmental stages, physical closeness and "I love you's" now
precipitate varying degrees of anxiety or real emotional discomfort.
It follows that as a teenage girl moves away from her father, she
moves toward the boy least like her father, emotionally and physically. The most likely choice, in most cases, once again being a bad
boy!

Case in point was my older daughter when she brought home her
first semi-serious boyfriend, Allen. If you haven't guessed by now,
I'm of medium height, slightly athletic build, and at that time had
a full head of black hair that was neatly styled. I definitely looked
Asian! No doubt about it.

Well, there I was sitting in the den quietly reading when the front doorbell chimes. Susan appears from her bedroom area and, in a mild state of excitement, runs to answer the doorbell. Minutes later, all smiles, she returns to the den with Allen.

Keeping me as a reference point, Allen stands slightly over six feet tall. Okay he's tall, taller than me anyway! He has shoulder-length straight blond hair and blue eyes. Oh, I forgot to tell you my eyes are brown. He has on a black T-shirt with the image of some sort of Rastafarian-looking fellow smoking what looks for all intents and purposes to be a joint. That shirt definitely wouldn't be my first or, for that matter, my last choice! His blue jeans are worn with multiple patched areas plus an open left knee area. And get this, he has on Vans, slip-on canvas-top, rubber-bottomed shoes. The canvas top of one shoe is a black and white checkerboard pattern and the other is a green, tan, and black camouflage. Now there's a sight for an Asian father's eyes! Before I could gasp or blurt out something that would have given away my shock and disgust—I mean disappointment—Susan chimed in, "Allen, this is my father, Dr. Tsao." A firm handshake associated with "It's really awesome to meet you. I mean really awesome. You know really, really awesome!" reflexively caused me to evaluate clinically that his IQ was probably somewhere below the median!

Truth be known, Allen was really an okay kid and quite smart, but being an experienced psychiatrist, I wasn't going to fall into the universally occurring parent trap that inevitably catches so many parents, particularly fathers. Instead of reacting instinctively and reactively, I was extremely gracious and friendly to Allen, even offering him a soda while we waited for Susan to finish preening before they left on their "Burger King and a movie" date.

Later when asked by Susan what I thought about Allen, I opined that I thought he was quite handsome, and with fingers crossed behind my back, further noted that they made "a really cute couple." Yuck! From that point forward, Allen was toast! Dr. Tsao was not about to let dating become the battleground or the struggle for my daughter's psychologically necessary separation-individuation developmental experience.

So often though, parents immediately overreact, making negative, prejudicial comments about the young man, and forbid their daughter from spending time, seeing, or communicating in any way with the young man. Big mistake! Huge!

First of all, the prohibitions are unenforceable. Come on now; with the mass and instant communication of cell phones, texting, Internet chat rooms, Facebook, or other personal sites on the Web, there is no feasible way to ensure that no communication or contact whatsoever will happen between them. I, by recent experience with my patients, have developed a very strong prejudice against text messaging. First of all, it is too available and too tempting to text during school hours. This becomes a real problem and detriment to the educational process. Although it is against the rules at most or all schools, the absolute silent aspect of this form of communication makes the school prohibition essentially unenforceable, especially related to those students seated midway and farther back in the classroom. Second, there is too much clandestine communication going on that the responsible adults will have no opportunity to eavesdrop upon either by chance or intention. For example, your child could be texting into the wee hours of the morning and, you would have no idea that this activity was going on. Texting has become the communication method of choice for drug dealers and the planning and institution of other unacceptable, illegal, and dangerous adolescent behaviors. And, last but not least, too many teenagers are texting while they're driving! For real, my patients have told me that they do it regularly. I've personally seen it while passing another vehicle that had been traveling erratically. As if driving while talking on the cell phone isn't dangerous enough already!

I have worked with very wealthy parents who sealed shut their daughter's bedroom windows from the outside! They installed sophisticated and complex security systems to keep the offensive boy away from their property, but of equal importance to keep their daughter securely sequestered inside the house! Despite all these efforts, with today's mobile and instant communication society, it just doesn't work. Sorry, but that's the cold, hard truth!

Second, the forbidden fruit is generally so temptingly sweet! Forbidding all contact will raise the boy to martyred hero status. He will become your daughter's "cause" to live. Don't turn your daughter and this guy into a Romeo and Juliet thing! The ultimate defeat and trauma for you, the parent, will be your daughter's stunning eventual proclamation, "I'm going to have his baby!" Yuck for sure!

For similar developmental, psychological, and hormonal reasons, this also happens with sons. For boys it is complicated by the idealized sexual object, which I will discuss later in much greater detail.

Mothers are usually stunned by their son's first serious girlfriend. Most mothers of teenage boys, whether they're the stay-at-home type or the working-outside-the-home type, generally don't have the time to invest in the latest fashions, hairstyles, and makeup. You're just too busy, burdened with too many responsibilities.

A local plastic surgeon's television ads corroborate this reality when the announcer hawks a free "mommy makeover" consultation because, "Only your children should see you as a mother!" Very catchy, I must say. However, after a couple of kids and the wear and tear of parenting, you probably should take advantage of the free consultation! So, just as girls will eventually start to feel some discomfort and as a result will distance themselves from their fathers, guys start to experience the same sort of feeling and are no longer comfortable with hugs and kisses from their mommy. It just "feels" somehow wrong. Therefore, with his testosterone levels rising, he is more and more attracted to the girls with the most estrogen, the "hoochie" girls! So, mom, be prepared for your now grown-up "little man" to bring home a girl who is clearly the number one contender to lead the Goths into battle or appears to have a promising future as a stripper or hooker!

The same advice applies: Don't immediately overreact. Don't make this the battleground of your son's adolescent separation-individuation struggle!

Often in therapy, when presented with this forbidden-fruit dilemma, I'll start by asking the teenager to tell me all the good and wonderful things about his or her significant other. I consciously and in a premeditated fashion develop a non-adversarial position. Nobody's perfect for sure. Over time the patient's forbidden-fruit boyfriend or girlfriend will mess up. Trust me. It's the nature of adolescents in particular and people in general to repeatedly mess up! However, rather than pounding away nonstop at his or her faults, as parents all too often do, despite my advice not to do such, I'll express my sympathy related to the particular transgression or indiscretion and ask my patient how it made him or her "really feel" when the problem occurred. It may take quite a number of indiscretions by the negative girlfriend or boyfriend, but over time, and through steady work, I usually get my patients to see the wisdom and personal value of "dumping" the negative significant other. I know we are headed in the right direction when my patient openly expresses his or her frustration with me, questioning why I insist on defending the multiple and repeated transgressions of the significant other when my patient has shared with me how much the behavior has so severely and deeply hurt him or her. Many a bad boy or hoochie girl has gone down in flames and had no idea that I was the man behind the scenes who launched the SAM missile that blew them up in mid flight!

Challenge number four, and probably the most important as it is the psychological framework intertwined with and underlying the previous challenges, is separation-individuation, a critical, absolutely necessary hurdle to be cleared if one is to ever be a healthy, functional adult.

Behaviorally it is typically exhibited in girls with a gradual or even abrupt shift in the confidentiality aspect of their relationship with their mother. Generally, prior to the teenage years, little girls can't wait to tell and share all their experiences and resultant feelings of the day with their mommy. They relish mom's feedback and approval. They readily share their most private, personal thoughts and feelings.

This all changes and evolves with adolescence. Sometimes it starts with something as simple or innocent as keeping a diary; this is behavior often actually encouraged by mom, who fondly remembers how much her own diary meant to her and the safe storage of her secret and most cherished thoughts, observations, and feelings. Sharing secrets, asking opinions, and reporting gossip now happen peer to peer, with mom being seen as much too old-fashioned and not up to speed, if not totally out of touch with today's life and its realities. In some ways this opinion held by the daughters may actually hold a grain of truth. Many parents have said to me while complaining in a somewhat self-righteous way, "I would have never thought to do what the kids are doing today." My counterpoint is, "You're absolutely right. If you had thought about it, you probably would've done it too"! Remember, try not to think about a polar bear. Okay then!

Our teens are under a constant barrage of mind-bending marketing. Radio, television, Internet, cell phones, print media, billboards, and malls are constantly and continuously pounding away, inserting the thoughts that if you are to be cool, accepted, or happy, you must have this hairstyle, this jewelry, these shoes, these clothes, this electronic device, etc. How can any child in today's society ever have all that the media says you absolutely must have in order to be happy? No way. They can't! Can any parent(s) realistically afford all these "material" things anyway? We now start to understand that if the child accepts this media-based standard—and thought insertion is truly irresistible and as a result they can't resist—it is then basically impossible for your daughter or son to ever be truly happy, based on the media-promulgated concept of happiness. And on top of this, when your child gets to high school he or she is thrown into the psychological jungle where with the slightest self-doubt or personal flaw, either real or imagined, your child will suffer terribly at the hands of his or her peers.

It's such a struggle to find and develop an acceptable self-face or self-image during adolescence. A lot of this should have been accomplished prior to this developmental time. Remember the drill instructor parent recommendation? Nonetheless this is exactly why your child will experiment with so many looks and personality styles—prep to gothic or grunge, Mohawk to shaved head, totally compliant to completely rebellious, "straight edge" to alcohol and drugs. This is all in an effort to find a comfort zone within themselves and in relationship to their peer group.

Specifically, for teenage girls, it's the resurfacing of the fairlytale world, "Mirror, mirror on the wall, who's the fairest of them all." Remember the bunny nation? It's all about competing for the attention of the alpha males. And how do girls compete? They do it by appearance and actions. They spend hours in front of the "mirror on the wall" hoping that the image they see or the answer they get is, "You are the fairest of them all." Yeah right! If the answer is that you are the fairest of them all, you probably suffer from grandiose delusions, or worse. If the mirror actually talks to you, then professional help involving a lot of heavy medication is clearly indicated!

The truth is that the mirror most often reveals all the flaws and imperfections of the answer seeker. The reflected image drives girls to purchase all kinds of makeup and hair products to improve their perceived attractiveness. They pick clothes that accentuate the positive and downplay the negative. They purchase fragrances that have the highest pheromone potential. Sadly, many girls, after spending so much time, effort, and energy, often give up in despair! Even worse off are the girls whose obsessions and compulsions progress to the development of eating disorders or other self-destructive behaviors.

Mirror devotion is further supported and driven by cheerleading tryouts. What a bind for the high school girl! It is announced over the school intercom for all to hear, and posted on various bulletin boards throughout the school, that cheerleading tryouts are about to begin.

Now, here's the bind. If you think you're good-looking enough to make the squad, then it's blatantly obvious you are a stuck-up "you know what" for sure! If you don't think you have what it takes, then you qualify for a free dog license at city hall because you must be such a woofer! If you don't try out, at least you can avoid the potential for public humiliation, a particular fear preventing many a young lady from even considering trying out.

Eventually, tryouts begin. Usually fifty to seventy-five girls and one guy show up. You kind of wonder about the one guy but are too busy and anxious yourself that you give it little further thought. You are called up in groups of three to show your "stuff" off in front of a group of teachers and the two senior co-captains of the current varsity squad. As you anxiously await your turn, you miraculously find religion and pray that the two other girls in your group either have some sort of physical disability or are clearly visibly deformed. Of course, no such luck! At the end of the day you are told that those still in the running will find their names posted on the bulletin board outside the school administration office in the morning. By the next morning, twenty-five names show up and about fifty girls go home sick! The list is further reduced until there only remains the "Miss America Twelve," and thirteen more girls go home sick! This ordeal not only selects the cheerleading squad, but it also has triggered many reactive serious depressive episodes, a percentage of which were associated with suicide gestures, attempts, or even suicides!

My suggestion more than twenty years ago to the superintendent of the local school district was to hold the tryout on a Friday, and get it over with. Pick the twelve "winners," and send everyone else home. This way there's no notice of winners and losers, no public humiliation, and the girls who don't make a spot on the varsity squad have the weekend to recover in the security of their family and their circle of close friends. They can even fabricate a face—saving story by Monday about how they were injured or really didn't feel well on Friday and either weren't able to perform to their full potential or to try out at all. It's not like I'm suggesting or endorsing lying, but when my suggested system was finally instituted years ago, the number of emergency-room visits related to overdoses and wrist cuttings causally related to cheerleading tryouts significantly decreased. Less work for shrinks and a decreased number of admissions to the psychiatric hospital, but more importantly the virtuous and right thing to do.

Even without cheerleading as a stimulus, the competition in adolescence is so keen that cruelty is the norm rather than the exception. I ask you, if four or five girls are gathered together at school or at the mall and are talking about another girl, even a so-called friend, who happens not to be present, what are the true odds they're saying something nice about her? Zero! Nada! No way!

The school system further endorses and promotes this experience by allowing cheerleaders to wear their uniforms with their school-colored cute tops and little short skirts to school, reinforcing for the other female students that they are just not up to standard, and definitely not hot!

The symbol of manhood or masculinity during my high school years was the varsity letter sweater. Let's take a short trip down memory lane together. It's true confession time. When I was in high school, I was a certified nerd! No question or doubt about it. I made straight A's, never caused trouble, was polite to a fault, and had absolutely no style whatsoever! I mean it! I was the typical Chinese/Asian son of immigrant parents. But I had one thing going for me. I could really run fast! I mean really fast. Now regardless of whether I developed this ability through the experience of outrunning bullies in grade school or I was just blessed with speed and athleticism, I was the fastest player in all the sports that I competed in during my high school years. As a result, despite being totally "uncool," I had status and respect because I wore my letter sweater to school with the embroidered little football within the larger school letter on the sweater. I know letter sweaters aren't important these days, but the tradition to some degree lives on in that most high schools allow or encourage the varsity football players to wear their game jerseys to school on game day. They show the rest of the school who the "real" men are, making all those without jerseys feel various degrees of inadequacy!

The importance of all this status stuff was clarified when my neighbor's son, who was a year ahead of me in high school, offered me his band sweater and forty bucks in exchange for my old football letter sweater. Even then I wasn't but so dumb. I took the forty dollars and told him he could keep the band sweater as I had no use for it! This is the kind of stuff I couldn't or wouldn't have shared with my dad for sure. He wouldn't have understood at all!

Where previously my dad had been my hero, I started wondering how I looked up to this man for so long as it was now clear as day to me that he didn't know zip about anything and was totally out of touch with my world! In fact he was, through no fault of his own. I often use this reality while working with my teenage patients. I point out that, in fact, their mother or father actually grew up in a totally different world that existed at least two decades ago or even longer than that. Therefore, the frame of reference related to the perception of reality for their mom and dad unquestionably has to be greatly different. I further clarify that the only reason I may seem to be up to speed with and understand their generation is because I spend so much time talking to their generation. I must confess that I'm actually starting to view rap and hip-hop as real or legitimate music! I must be working too hard!

I also try to get my patients to see the flip side of the coin, that their parents, despite all the put-downs and negative critiques, seem to be getting along just fine, that their perception of reality, wrong or old-fashioned as it may seem to the teenager, "works" for their parents. After all it's the teenager who's the one in therapy!

To further clarify the struggle for high school girls, you would have to look at high school boys. If you were to conduct a confidential survey, asking the boys to name the one girl in school with whom they would most want to have a date, about five to ten girls would get all the votes, meaning the rest of the hundreds of girls at the school are obviously second rate or just plain chopped liver! And how or on what basis do the boys make their selection?

The process starts years prior to adolescence. Around the age of nine to ten, boys start to input data and information into the hard drive of their minds, formatting their ideal sexual object, their perfect sexual woman so to speak. This process and the idealized sexual object are basically completed by around thirteen to sixteen years of age with little refinements and adjustments done in the years that follow. In today's society a major source of soft-core sexual material is actually delivered free of charge to your home on a monthly basis, if not more frequently: the Victoria's Secret catalog. Mothers often tell me that the catalog mysteriously disappears before she even gets a chance to look through it, the missing issue being later discovered somewhere in her son's possession, hidden in a secret place. If not Victoria's Secret, there's still Playboy, Penthouse, Hustler, late-night television, and, almost universally available, the Internet.

Boys are continuously thought inserting this material and putting together the visual and psychological woman of their ultimate sexual fantasies. You don't have to have a great imagination to get the picture! This ideal sexual woman has to have a beautiful, sensuous face and an unrealistically—because it's not real—fantastic sexy body and the psychological personality makeup that she is driven to please the man and always wants and can never get enough sex—in effect, an absolutely gorgeous nymphomaniac! Understanding this, you start to comprehend why all of the boys vote purely on the basis of looks and you gain a little insight as to why girls are so driven to look the best they can, and the sexiest, either consciously or intuitively understanding this about boys and men.

Therefore, the necessity for a training bra or push-up bra is obvious, because they look so good on the models in Victoria's Secret—and don't forget what we discussed about the emotional importance of breasts in chapter 1. Besides, the catalog is the source of most of the guys' fantasies initially. So, all the better to mimic as closely as possible the images as presented in the catalogs. Full makeup, dyed hair, and the most revealing clothes are all part of the teen-age girl's response. Just look around when you're out and about, and you'll see what I'm talking about. How else do you explain, as noted in chapter 1, that about 336,000 American girls, age eighteen or younger, according to an AMA report, had breast augmentations in the year 2006. That number was anticipated to be significantly higher for 2007, approaching half a million nationally! Whether or not you consider breast augmentation or "boob jobs" to be a societal problem, there are much more serious things to consider in this chapter.

First, understanding that hormonal increase and sexual drive are undirected and without object to start out with, then it follows that it is important to see the clear and present danger of child pornography or similar sexual material easily being available on the Internet and through other media resources or outlets. It also shouts loudly to the critical need to eliminate child pornography altogether! Consider what the results will be if a young man's initial sexuality and orgasmic fulfillment is formatted by viewing child pornography. Really think about. Remembering that you never get a second chance to make a first impression, and in this instance a lasting if not lifelong impression, plus understanding the irresistibility of thought insertion, you don't want a little boy's first sexual chance impression about human sexuality to be that of sex with children. Men, when you take into account how truly fixed your own sexualized object is and how basically unchangeable over time it has become, then it is undeniable that exposure to child pornography can only create more child sexual predators. It also speaks volumes as to why sexual predators are so difficult to treat or to rehabilitate, if change is even actually possible.

Similar to this dangerous negative outcome has been the emotional fallout and sexual identity confusion for the victims of predators. I've had the rather unique experience of working with two heterosexual youngsters who, prior to being victimized by sexual predators, neither expressed nor exhibited any problem with their sexual orientation or choice of girlfriend or boyfriend.

In the first case, my male patient of preadolescent age was in treatment related to family conflict and dysfunction. Coincidentally during his therapy related to his family problems, this young man was targeted by a grown man whose choice of victims happened to be preadolescent boys. The predator male accosted my patient in the locker room of a public facility and frightened and threatened him to be quiet and cooperate. The involuntary cooperation of my patient established, the predator engaged in various perverted sexual acts with my patient's genitals. Eventually, the predator was arrested, charged, and convicted of his crime against my patient. The frightening truth is that my patient was far from his only victim, but thankfully his "last" until he is released from prison, should he ever make it to his release date. The emotional fallout for this particular young man was years of questioning and self-doubt, very real emotional suffering. He wondered why this man "specifically" singled him out. Was there something about him that attracted this predator to him? He worried about and questioned if he had some homosexual characteristics that resulted in this assault. Was he, in even some small way, to blame? Was he somehow complicit in the events that transpired? He also felt a great sense of guilt and shame that the actions of the perverted man had at some level aroused him sexually. It took years of intensive therapy for him to accept and feel comfortable with his own heterosexuality.

My second example is the story of an adolescent girl who was also struggling with significant family dysfunction. She had many boyfriends prior to getting involved in her first serious, intensely "in love" relationship. Her boyfriend was about three and a half years her senior and showered her with gifts, time, and attention, all the more seductive related to her ongoing conflict with her parents. Although her parents clearly expressed their complete and total censure against the relationship with this "boy" due to the age disparity and many other legitimate reasons, they carried on their "love" for each other and the intimacies of their relationship in secret. When the clandestine relationship was finally and explosively exposed after an overnight runaway episode that involved the police, it was discovered that my patient's boyfriend was in truth a transvestite/transsexual, the "he" was in fact a "she." She was a sexual predator just like the man who molested my young male patient. The young woman was shocked and confused. It once again took years of treatment to overcome her feelings of self-doubt and guilt related to "falling in love" with a woman and having experienced such intense sexual arousal and feelings, yet another victim of sexual predation. The moral of this story is that parents and society must be aware of this danger to their children and are obligated to take all reasonable precautions to protect their loved ones.

The second societal/legal problem related to all of this goes back to high school and the five to ten girls who got all the votes. That there were just five to ten is the problem! They are the focus of fantasy and emotion for the hundreds of boys in the school. Bad odds! But that doesn't stop every young man, tall or short, over-weight or underweight, normal or handicapped, rich or poor fam-ily, from wanting to be the boyfriend of one of the "Barbie" choices. In fact, the Barbies are showered with gifts, flowers, and poetry by secret admirers and some not so secret.

The hard truth is that the hundreds of boys really have no chance! Most of the Barbies are already seeing older, more accomplished guys already in college or established in their careers. Sometimes, by various means and manipulations, a teenage boy may even reach the status of "friend" with one of the Barbies, only to suffer that much more over time because the unobtainable desired object is so very, very close and yet so very, very far away that she might as well be in the next galaxy! Over time, the futile and emotionally painful effort of "Cher Cher La Femme" and the resultant frustration can and eventually does lead to frustration and anger.

Boys often start, and this can happen fairly early on, to see the "hot" girls as just a bunch of bitchy "teases." It has been well-estab-lished that rape is an act of anger, not sex. Where do you think that anger originates? Now you know! How many young men's efforts to be involved with their fantasized girl are destroyed on the rocks of adolescence, their self-esteem severely crushed because of the siren's seductive call, a combination of the scarcity of truly hot girls and the young man's own internalized, idealized sexual object. Be-yond rape itself, this psychological truth is also played out in other deviant sexual behaviors—from flashing to various levels of moles-tation, from touching and fondling to penetration, lingual to digital, everything up to and just short of rape itself. Once again the power of the idealized sexual image raises its ugly head.

Based on what you have now learned and understand, which group of girls do you think these deviant men tend to focus most of their energies intensively upon? So, you can see that being one of the best-looking girls around, although wished for and sought after by all young women, can also be a great liability, these beautiful girls more often becoming the recipients of as much or more negative pathologic attention than positive. Just ask any really beautiful woman; if she's honest, she'll tell you that what I've elucidated is absolutely the truth. This negative attention and interaction with men can often lead to significant negative emotional fallout for even these sought-after and adored women.

The proof of all this and the extremely painful struggle of adolescence and its consequences were exemplified in the life of a young man I worked with now decades ago. I became his psychiatrist after he had made a true and serious suicide attempt by hanging and was admitted to the psychiatric hospital to recover from the attempt and to ensure his own safety. He was fifteen at the time and had clearly given up on life. He still had the physical evidence of his attempted suicide, clear and obvious bruising circling his neck.

Now Eddie, as I'll call him for confidentiality reasons, had reason, at least in his mind, to give up on living. He candidly told me that he, in fact, was disappointed that he had not ended his "miserable" life.

Eddie suffered from mild cerebral palsy that affected his right side, causing him to have limited use of his right hand, arm, and leg. This disability resulted in his carrying his affected hand in a drop position and also caused him to drag his right foot to some degree, making normal ambulation basically impossible and painfully slow. The palsy also caused some speech impediment in terms of minimal slurring and was probably also somehow causally related to his lazy eye condition that had less than complete recovery after multiple corrective surgeries. The reality was that his eye still didn't look quite right and he knew it. For years he had been the object of hurtful derogatory statements, rejection by peers, and diverted gazes from adults. As if that wasn't bad enough, he also suffered with ADD and was failing academically.

When I was randomly assigned to be Eddie's psychiatrist, he was able, despite his mild speech impediment, to clearly and logically express all of his reasons why life was so painful and intolerable, that the only reasonable alternative to stop all the interminable pain was to commit suicide.

I told Eddie I wasn't a magician or illusionist, that I could not change the realities of his life and what he had been through. However, I did tell him that I believed I could and would try to help him to the best of my ability.

I started him on what was then a new antidepressant, fluoxetine hydrochloride (Prozac), plus what was also new then, the longer-acting stimulant, Ritalin SR. Within four weeks Eddie was feeling better in terms of his overall mood and eventually his academic performance at school had also dramatically improved. In fact, his academic performance was so much improved that he was "mainstreamed" out of special education back into his originally assigned high school.

Good start. But not so fast! When Eddie was in Special Ed, he was just one of the menagerie of disabled students. Special Ed doesn't mean that you're "special." In fact, it means just the opposite and all the kids know it. When Eddie did attend the Special Education school, he quietly blended in with the crowd. He was in a sense safe. Not so back at his regular high school. He became, once again, the lightning rod for the cruelty that abounds in adolescence.

When he showed up mid semester at his zoned high school, he was not only the new student but the new "handicapped" student, easy prey. Because of his mild cerebral palsy and resultant right-sided disabilities, residual lazy eye, and somewhat slurred speech, he had nowhere to hide! He was totally rejected socially, isolated. Name-calling included "Retard, Quasimodo, Igor, Hunchback." He shuffled along the halls, head bowed. He ate lunch alone every day outside the school cafeteria away from all other students. No one talked to him on the school bus, unless to make fun of or to mock him. He tearfully shared his pain with me during our many therapy sessions. I shared his hurt internally but always remained positive externally. How could I not relate to Eddie's feelings about being a rejected outsider, having experienced prejudice up close and personal myself as a youngster, my early years spent living in Harlem, New York? Using positive thought insertion as a therapeutic tool, I always pointed out his positive traits and accomplishments. I pointed to the future and confidently noted that there was surely "life" after high school.

Based on information shared that he did go to church now and then with his mother, I asked at one point in his treatment whether there was a youth group at his mother's church. I suggested that if there was one, he should look into it. Eddie's mother's church was very small and didn't have an established youth program, but the pastor told him of a Young Life group at another church that was reasonably close by. Even with my suggestions and pushing, it took months for Eddie to actually attend one of those Young Life meetings. He openly and honestly expressed that his fear of rejection was the biggest factor holding him back.

Then a miracle happened! Whether due to my efforts in our sessions or some sort of divine intervention, he reluctantly attended a Young Life meeting. He couldn't wait to tell me, "Dr. Tsao, I think they like me." After a tearful, thoughtful pause: "At least they didn't hurt me." Those Young Life kids did as much for Eddie as I could have ever accomplished without their help, possibly even more. One of the youth group's members actually attended Eddie's high school. He became Eddie's friend. He made contact every day and made it a point to walk with him along the halls, in some way I suspect to shield Eddie from the daily hurts that he had experienced all too often at the hands of the other students. They sat together every day in the cafeteria and broke bread together.

When the youth group went on excursions, like to a local theme park, they walked, as a group, more slowly so that Eddie wouldn't fall behind. They invited Eddie to attend Christian summer camp, and he actually went twice. Eddie had a life!

At the start of his senior year, Eddie had gained enough self-confidence and courage that he was going to get a job. He wanted so much to have a car of his own. Over the next month or so he applied to twenty or more local businesses. Their response was, to say the least, underwhelming as he didn't even get the courtesy of a response to his initial round of applications. That got me really fired up! I was mad! Eddie was crestfallen over the rejections, further reinforcing his ingrained feeling of worthlessness. At that juncture, I anonymously and personally got involved and called the local fast-food restaurant that was closest to Eddie's home, knowing that he could walk to work if hired. I spoke to the manager, reminding him that it was illegal to discriminate against hiring people with disabilities. He initially denied that that was ever the case at his store. I knew this wasn't true as Eddie had told me he had specifically applied, at least twice, at that particular restaurant. Finally, with my pushing, the manager agreed to consider anybody that I might send by who was looking for work. Eddie got the job!

Unfortunately, because of his handicaps, he was not able to work the cash register or handle the cooking of the food. He got the most menial job: mopping the floors, cleaning and wiping down the tables and chairs, emptying the trash units, and cleaning the bathrooms. He never once complained though. In fact, he took great pride in his work, and often told me how spotless and clean the bathrooms were when he was done with his shift. He eventually became the most reliable employee of that restaurant, never being tardy or missing work despite the fact that he had to walk to work, regardless of good or bad weather. He did eventually get that used car he had so much wanted.

It was now the spring of Eddie's senior year, and all was going well. I had discontinued his Prozac. His mood remained stable without the reemergence of any suicidal thoughts. He still needed his stimulant medication to address his ADD and academic performance. Unfortunately, the oft-painful struggle of adolescence raised its ugly head one more time.

Senior year means senior prom! All seniors, because of this event, are forced to take a serious look at themselves and their self-face whether they like it or not. Eddie was no exception. Despite all his handicaps, Eddie, not unlike every other guy his age, had a fixed idealized woman of his dreams formatted in the hard drive of his mind. Like every other young man he wanted and needed a date for prom. It forced Eddie to really look at himself and his self-worth in our therapy sessions.

As the prom approached, he became more and more disturbed and self-denigrating. Then another miracle! Out of the blue one of the best-looking, hot girls in his Young Life group approached him and asked if he was planning to attend his senior prom. When Eddie told her sadly that it wasn't looking good, she told him that she would be "honored" to be his date!

After his senior prom, Eddie proudly showed me his prom picture. There he was, all decked out in his tuxedo with a red bow tie, and on his left good arm was this absolutely gorgeous young lady in a blue satin gown. She had on a lovely wrist corsage, proudly paid for by Eddie. They were both smiling. Eddie told me they had a wonderful time at the prom. He proudly shared with me that he was sure that every other guy there was envious of "my" date. Like many other couples, they even went to breakfast together after the prom. While proudly showing me the prom picture, Eddie, through his somewhat slurred speech, noted, "Dr. Tsao, I'm so happy. For once in my life I had the most beautiful girl as my date. I'll never forget it." But then, the hard, painful truth: "But I know she don't like me like that; she's just a good Christian girl." He went on to further state optimistically, "But I can still dream, can't I"? Of course you can, Eddie. We all need to dream. Without dreams there is no hope and no future.

Eddie graduated on time with his senior class, a moment of great triumph for the human spirit. Attired in his cap and gown like every other graduate, when it was his turn, he shuffled across the stage while the entire senior class including those who had rejected and ridiculed him for so many painful years rose as one and applauded. I, with a tear of joy, did the same.

The last I heard was that Eddie went on to a Bible college with the intent to someday become a minister. I haven't heard from him or his family for decades now, but I must say that my life was made so much better, so much more enriched for the opportunity to have shared a few miles on the highway of life with Eddie. As much as I believe that I have given all I had to give to the thousands of patients, my "kids" as I like to call them all, they've all given so much more back to me.

Adolescence is an overwhelming life experience for every child, and I mean every child. The adolescent, like it or not, willing or screaming and kicking all the way, in some way, shape, or form, will have to measure up. Parental support and love alone won't be sufficient to carry them through. By graduation, there will be one valedictorian and one salutatorian, and the rest of the graduating class will be just numbers. The yearbook will herald the "best looking," "most likely to succeed," "most artistic," and "most athletic." How does this make the other graduates feel? Not good, I can tell you! All this just confirms their lack of self-worth.

Always keeping my "leaf in the stream" analogy in mind, I point out to the kids I have had the opportunity to work with that in order to be happy, you don't have to follow the same path as everyone else. It just matters if you are the best that you can be in whatever you endeavor to do. Eddie, despite what others might have felt about his job, was really proud of those bathrooms! I supported him 100 percent related to his sense of pride. It's important that parents try to do what I did for Eddie. Identify the good and positive things about your child or adolescent. Support the positive things with your time and effort. Tell them that you're proud of their accomplishments no matter how big or how small. Tell them that you love them. Be there and comfort them when they fail, as they often will. Do all this, and your child will truly feel and know that you are a good and loving parent.

I must admit that, probably related to my own Chinese background, I'm guilty of pushing my patients pretty hard about education. I had a particularly good time doing therapy when a young man who was slacking off in school told me he didn't need to know physics or chemistry, "cause I'm gonna grow up to be" an auto technician working on race cars or fantasy cars.

My counterpoint was to ask this young man to explain to me why a car goes faster when you depress the accelerator pedal, the answer not being that the mice run faster, what's the difference between supercharging and turbocharging, or the difference between fuel injection versus carburetion. I asked why it is an advantage to have four valves per cylinder rather than two or what impact on performance is related to the coefficient of drag, all of which he would know and understand better if he had listened in geometry, chemistry, and physics.

Finally, and this is usually the killer eye-opener, I ask that if he was lucky and successful enough to own the new 600-plus horsepower Corvette or Shelby Cobra, should he happen to be a Ford guy, would he want the technician working on his "super" car to have made straight A's or the C's and D's that his current report card documented. He got the point! Then it is my job to build from there. In short, sometimes adolescent psychotherapy can actually be a lot of fun and usually very, very rewarding when effective!

However, let's get back to the separation-individuation discussion. The point here is that it is important to let your kid win. Let me say it again: It's important to let your kid win. Now, if you yourself are a very competitive person, this may be a hard thing to do. But if you listen to me, you'll be the "real" winner in the long run. Remember, I cautioned earlier that you don't want the separation-individuation battleground to be education, behavior, sex, or any other area that you really care about. It may naturally or spontaneously occur if you're lucky and observant, or if not so lucky, then it's up to you to consciously pick the field of battle, to draw the line in the sand.

For example, living in southeastern Virginia, the boys in this area generally grow up to be devoted, die-hard Washington Redskins fans. My suggestion to their fathers over the years has been to become a devoted Dallas Cowboys fan. This will confirm for your son that which he already now believes to be true, that you really are stupid and definitely out of touch with reality!

Totally enjoy the fray which is sure to ensue as to which is really the "better" football team. Purchase Cowboys jerseys and caps. Emphasize that the Cowboys cheerleaders are really "hot" and reign over the Redskin cheerleaders. Fight to the bitter end, keeping in mind that it really doesn't matter to you which team eventually wins, or at least I hope not!

I'll use an example from many years ago to illustrate this point. A very educated, professional couple brought their sixteen-year-old son to me for help. They were in a pitch battle over study habits, grades, and school dress code. Their son was a junior at a local prep school, and, despite a tested IQ somewhere well above 130, he was now making C's and was often sent home for dress code violations. They'd come down hard on him in regard to discipline and restrictions, all to no avail. It was the irresistible force versus the immovable object. They were at their wit's end! They finally brought Will (a fictitious name) to see me.

After several initial sessions I evaluated that Will was a pretty good kid after all, with no significant psychiatric disorder, but was in the typical adolescent separation-individuation battle with his parents, who themselves were not willing to give an inch on anything. Neither was Will!

During one of our many therapy sessions in the spring, he shared with me that he loved the Cincinnati Reds baseball team. Here was my opening! Remember how much I love baseball? Opportunity was clearly knocking. He asked me if I knew much about his team. I premeditatedly responded that I thought that the Reds were a "pathetic excuse" for a major league baseball club. Will was shocked, disappointed, and mad! He challenged me with whether I thought I knew a better team, and I picked the Pittsburgh Pirates. He exasperatedly stated that he couldn't believe that here he thought I was a pretty cool, understanding doctor, and now he finds out that I think the Pirates are a better team than his Reds. The battle was joined! We debated, heatedly at times, which was really the better team. By the end of the season Cincinnati had won more games than Pittsburgh, and Will brought in the local paper's sports section with the final National League Central standings. He triumphantly rubbed in my face the fact that "my" Reds finished above "your" Pirates. He had won! Now, of course, I did a lot of other therapeutic work with Will, but the end result was that he was making straight A's once again and was no longer bucking the dress code at his school. His parents were very pleased and amazed at the positive turnaround that had occurred.

During the exit interview they wondered aloud how I was ever able to change their son's behavior so much to the positive in almost all areas of his life! Since they probably never would have understood and were not in the mental health field, I never did tell them about the Reds and the Pirates. Will eventually went on to medical school and became a physician. I bet he still loves his Reds!

Closer to home I picked the piano for my battleground. My wife believed that playing the piano was a cultural and good thing for our older daughter, Susan. Now, mind you, not just any piano, but a Steinway! After having the wife of one of my colleagues, who was herself an accomplished concert pianist, pick out the best piano, we started the process of piano lessons. Susie was actually quite gifted. However, when she reached her teens, many other things, in her mind at least, took precedence over the Steinway.

I seized the opportunity presented, as I would have done in my therapeutic work, and got after Susan to devote more time and energy to practicing. She resisted and the battle was joined! I would constantly remind her to practice, noting that the piano looked "lonely" and was just a waste of good money since she was no longer keeping up with her practice and playing.

She fought me all the way. She eventually defiantly took the position that she was no longer going to practice nor participate in any future piano recitals, ever again. It was great! She won and secretly I, of course, didn't care! She remained an honor student, didn't marry Alan, didn't get in trouble with alcohol, drugs, or the police, and is the mother of my precious granddaughters, plus is a practicing child psychologist and school psychologist in Massachusetts. The Steinway rests to this day in storage, silent testimony to letting your adolescent win sometime is psychologically necessary and can truly be effective parenting.

If through our discussion you have come to see how difficult and challenging adolescence can be, then think about throwing one more straw on the proverbial burdened camel's back, this last stress possibly being the straw that brings the camel to its knees. You or your child has gone through or is going through the crucible of the teenage years, investing so much time and energy trying to establish a self-face you can like or accept within yourself, while simultaneously developing an acceptable face you can present to the world at large. It follows then that you want to, figuratively or literally, put your "best" face forward at this time of your life.

How may I ask can an adolescent put forth his or her "literal" best face forward when it's covered with zits—blemishes, pimples, pustules, craters, acne!

Up until adolescence, children generally have such lovely, radiant, "peaches and cream" complexions. Then as the world-famous chef Emeril says, "Bam! There they are!" "Yeah, baby!" Zits! They could not have chosen a worse time to show up. While the guys gaze into the mirror every morning urgently hoping to see if they're growing a beard yet, they start to see bumps that enlarge, redden, and like small volcanoes eventually spew white yucky stuff. The girls, now devotedly committed to the reawakening of the "mirror, mirror on the wall" phenomenon, get the unwanted answer: "For certain it's not you with those ugly things on your face." Yuck!

The cause underpinning the arrival for this unwanted cutaneous event is hormones once again. As sex hormones advance, they cause a change in the physiology of the teenager's skin. For those unfortunate teens with a propensity or predisposition to develop acne, this is when it will happen or will get significantly worse. This is further documented by the fact that girls who are taking birth control pills often need to switch types or adjust dosages because of such skin problems. The phenomenon is seen with guys as generally the last boys needing to shave tend to have the better complexions. Lucky me! Remember I'm one of those relatively hairless Asian guys.

As with many aspects of adolescence, there is misinformation and misunderstanding that passes from generation to generation. For example, while attending a Catholic prep school, I was instructed that pimples were the outward sign of our dirty sexual inner thoughts and related frequency of masturbatory activity. Great! As a teen, you could always feel when a pimple was about to emerge or was actively emerging. So there I was, my father asking me to pass the green beans, and the zit is emerging on my nose. I'm pretty sure that my father can see what kind of thoughts I've been having lately!

As I've grown older and wiser, I have wondered how Father Purcell could have disseminated such pure and unadulterated bunk. Actually, now that I have become a well-educated and trained physician and psychiatrist, I have come to see where Father Purcell might have been actually right, but for the "wrong" reasons! It's sex hormone that changes the physiology of your skin allowing the development of pimples. In the case of boys, testosterone also initiates and develops male sexuality with resultant increased sexual thoughts and related masturbatory activity. Therefore, the common denominator cause of blemishes and masturbation is hormones, not that masturbation and sexual thoughts are truly causally related to the emergence of zits!

The other misinformation or lie told to teenagers is that zits will go away once you reach adulthood. If zits are related to the levels of sex hormone, then what is the logic of their disappearance by age eighteen to twenty-one? There is no logic here! As long as you have active sex hormones, you'll still get zits!

Physiologically, sex hormones do decrease over time as seen in both men and women. A woman's menopause is much more obvious and generally occurs chronologically earlier, but the hormonal decline does also occur for men. Sorry, guys, hard fact, scientific truth! Thus the widespread need for and prescription of Viagra can be scientifically explained. Come on, guys, you know it's true. Using myself as an example of a man being in his late sixties, due to my now being on the downward slope, hopefully not the slippery slope of aging, associated with a decrease in testosterone production, my face is finally pimple free. Ah! Other than a few wrinkles, my skin looks pretty good now. Unfortunately, although I look better in terms of no blemishes, I've got nothing to back up my better-looking skin! Bummer, getting older isn't much fun after all. Maybe the golden years aren't really so golden. I'm sure that all this explains the financial success and the psychological need for drugs like the previously mentioned Viagra.

Once again on a more serious note, parents should be aware of and sensitive to this issue for their teens. Invest in skin products. Take your teenager to your family doctor or dermatologist for medical intervention, if necessary. You may even want to consider Accutane as a last resort if your child's acne is not responsive to less invasive or drastic measures. Your child will appreciate your time and effort and will feel so much better about themselves overall when they have a clearer complexion and can literally put their best face forward.

Once one fully comprehends the magnitude and the multifaceted stressors of adolescence and its documented high rate of emotional meltdowns and suicides, it further emphasizes and documents the need for each child, particularly your child, to have something, anything about themselves that they can be proud of or believe in so that under the emotional pressure and stresses of this time of their life, they have something solid they can truly fall back on emotionally.

This is the reason why the involvement in real-time, real-world activities before the onset of adolescence is so very critical. Facing this dangerous stretch of life's highway with the road ahead strewn with deep potholes, sharp turns, hazards, and IEDs, your child needs strong emotional body armor. They are going to take many direct and an equal or greater number of glancing blows to the heart of their psyche during this emotionally unstable and turbulent time. The result of all this emotionally is that adolescence, with its inherent stresses, is the time when if a person has a genetic predisposition associated with one of the major psychiatric disorders like

Schizophrenia or Bipolar Disorder, then this will be the time of the first "nervous breakdown" or major "regression."

In fact, from a statistical standpoint, if you haven't experienced a major emotional breakdown during your teens or early adult life, then the odds are greatly in your favor that you never will, except in the case of extraordinary circumstance.

Based on all that we have now learned together about adolescence, is it any wonder that so many teenagers become depressed and make suicide gestures or attempts by the hundreds of thousands annually, with actually tens of thousands tragically ending their lives? I should point out that during the teenage years, suicide has statistically been most often causally related to the perceived or actual loss of a girlfriend or boyfriend. Since this is such a frequent occurrence throughout the adolescent years, one can see the very real high potential risk. Please be aware of this particular loss for your teenager. Obviously, there are so, so many potholes and accidents along the highway of adolescent life beyond loss of girlfriend or boyfriend that are painful and disabling enough to push a teen to the brink of suicide or beyond. If you throw a family genetic history of suicide into the mix, it can be a deadly combination foretelling a tragic, fatal ending to the story.

Armed with understanding, experience, and training, a competent therapist can help your child. But, therapy alone may not be enough!

Related to the concept of a comprehensive treatment approach, I'd like to take a little time and talk about fluoxetine hydrochloride, Prozac. That's right, Prozac! Fluoxetine hydrochloride is its chemical or generic name.

Now I know that there has been massive controversy recently related to the prescription of antidepressant drugs to children, a child by definition being anyone younger than eighteen years of age. It is my opinion that the media—by its hyped focus on antidepressants potentially increasing "suicidal thoughts" in children, as noted by the FDA in its "black box warning"—was committing a great public disservice. Keep in mind that the warning was for "suicidal thoughts" only and not suicidal "action." The reaction to the "front page" press releases either in print or through television exposure caused many parents to stop their children's prescribed antidepressants for fear that the child would become "suicidal." Some of my patients' parents were no exception. The sad and tragic result of this drop in the prescription of or the frank non-compliance to the administration of antidepressant medications and the general over-all parental resistance to giving such medications to their children was a resultant AMA-reported increase in childhood "suicides" of more than 35,000 children during the next twelve months! A recent newspaper article reported that the teen suicide rate remains sig-nificantly elevated over previous recorded years and levels, all since the frenzied media hawking of the so-called "black box warning." These very important and statistically significant reports about the increased number of actual teenage suicides and their ongoing ex-istence unfortunately never made it to the front page.

My analogy has consistently been that for years doctors have treated pneumonia with penicillin or penicillin family drugs, but a significant number of people didn't get better and died from their contracted pneumonia. A number of people even died as result of an allergic reaction to the penicillin itself! Based on this knowledge, should physicians stop prescribing any and all antibiotics to treat pneumonia? How can it be that the penicillin did not work, and in some cases was the cause of an adverse reaction, like anaphylactic shock or even death?

The medical answer to this question is because all pneumonias aren't caused by the same bacteria or virus. Similarly, not all de-pressions have the same root cause for their appearance. Therefore, the need for different types of antibiotics and an equivalent need for different types of antidepressants or therapies becomes clearly and logically obvious. In fact, this in truth is the medical reality.

My other point in this area of psychiatric treatment is that phy-sicians and psychiatrists prescribe antidepressants to people who are "depressed." Duh! Depressed people, as a direct and proximal cause related to their depression or depressed mood, will sustain the feeling or belief that life's just not worth living, and it follows logically that they will develop suicidal thoughts, plans, and may even attempt to carry out these self-destructive plans just as Eddie did!

Well-trained mental health professionals have long been taught that the most potentially dangerous time in treating a depressed patient is when they start feeling better, the concept being that when they're the most severely debilitated with depression, they don't have enough energy to make an actual suicide attempt. So it follows logically that when a person is started on an antidepressant and feeling better, associated with more "energy," they will be at a greater risk to act on their suicidal thoughts, if still present. Psychiatrist, therapist, family, and friends should be aware of the risk of this phenomenon and be extremely cautious and vigilant to its possible existence.

It just doesn't make any sense to me not to treat with antidepressants because this reaction might occur in the course of recovery. For more than 35,000 deceased kids last year, it doesn't really matter anymore, does it?

So why use Prozac for kids? First of all, Prozac and Zoloft are the only medications in their class, selective serotonin reuptake inhibitors or SSRIs, that are approved by the FDA for prescription to children. Second, there are hundreds, if not thousands, of published studies documenting the safety and efficacy of Prozac. Third, hundreds of millions of people have taken Prozac over the last twenty-two years, and no untoward side effects have really been discovered. Finally, it's safe! Prozac is non-addictive and non-habituative, and because of this it can be started or stopped at any time without any problems like withdrawal. Its allergic reaction rate is close to if not better than that of acetaminophen, Tylenol. I've never actually seen an allergic reaction to Prozac. In addition, it is one of the few drugs that the FDA has evaluated as safe for pregnant women or those who are breast-feeding to take. How good is that! A physician is not required to do blood tests, a urinalysis, cardiogram, or EEG, as Prozac has no known significant negative impact on heart, kidney, liver, lung, or brain function. On top of all this, it's easy to dose, usually twenty to forty milligrams once a day being effective. Knowing all this, what reason could there be to withhold it from children who are suffering with a potentially "terminal" depression? Even money or expense can't be a deterrent as recent television ads promote that Wal-Mart pharmacies charge only twelve dollars for ninety capsules, basically a three-month supply for only twelve bucks!

In explaining all this recently, I point out to my patients and their parents, as I've mentioned earlier in this discussion, that during the fall of 2006 the British published the results of a study of major scientific significance to the treatment of children suffering with depression. The results of the study showed that with at least twelve months of taking their prescribed fluoxetine every day, that brain imaging studies done at the study's end demonstrated that the children's brains actually had developed new serotonin neurons or brain cells, a process known as "neurogenesis," in effect pointing to Prozac actually having a potential long-term "curative effect" if taken for at least one year. The idea is that if children have a positive clinical response to Prozac, they might be potentially "cured" and may never have to take an antidepressant again! Is that awesome or what?

Recall also my discussion on ADD/ADHD where I said that some of the genetics pointed to some possible serotonin dysfunction over time. Serotonin deficit or deficiency is related behaviorally to impulsivity, depression, anger, and aggression. This is why I often add Prozac to the prescribed stimulant medication to address this issue should it arise, which it often does. I have talked about this use of Prozac in the overall treatment of ADD/ADHD for years now in my seminars to thousands of physicians around this great land. It has personally been most gratifying to get feedback from so many of them reporting such great success when they added Prozac to the already prescribed stimulant ADD/ADHD medication.

Allow me to more clearly explain. During my many lectures and discussions, I've pointed out a phenomenon or occurrence that all physicians who treat ADD/ADHD have experienced. After properly diagnosing the child or adolescent, the usual response to the initial prescription of stimulants is quite good, if not excellent. In fact, as has been documented in published medical literature, the probable good to excellent combined response rate between methylphenidate- or amphetamine-based products is 92 percent. However, after a period of time that generally ranges from six months to thirty-six months, the treated youngster may start to exhibit some often disturbing behavioral patterns that usually take the form of moodiness, edginess, decreased socialization, easy loss of temper, anger, and even what appear to be unprovoked aggressive episodes. Basically the thousands of doctors I have discussed this phenomenon with have agreed with its frequency of occurrence and the negative impact of its existence. They admit that the usual clinical response is to adjust the dose, usually upward, of the stimulant medication or switch methylphenidate to amphetamine or vice versa. They may add clonidine or guanfacine; consider adding Strattera, Risperdal, or Seroquel to the total medication regimen.

With further discussion and frank honesty, the doctors usually admit that these attempted changes meet with minimal to no real clinical success or significant behavioral improvement. With little to no positive clinical response, the non-psychiatrist physicians usually then refer the patient to a psychiatrist.

However, it has been my contention for years that ADD/ADHD should not necessarily be treated by psychiatrists in the first place or on an ongoing basis since in its basic form it is simply a less-than-normal ability to pay attention; and this condition can be more than adequately treated by pediatricians, family physicians, and nurse practitioners.

My Prozac recommendation is based on the aforementioned genetics. Please note that the IMAGE project, as headed by Dr. Stephen Faraone, has identified the group of candidate genes that lead to the syndrome of ADD/ADHD. The first five genes that have been elucidated affect dopamine and norepinephrine function; and therefore, this ADD/ADHD person logically and scientifically should respond well to one of the stimulant medications. The remaining one or two genes elucidated affect serotonin function; and, therefore, they should respond to the prescription of Prozac or Zoloft. The question that quite naturally follows is why doesn't the serotonin dysfunction associated with its behavioral and mood problems simultaneously occur with that of dopamine and norepinephrine dysfunctions? My explanation is that it's genetic expression timing. So many mothers have told me their child in particular was "hyperactive" in utero, while "in my belly," demonstrating that the inattention and/or hyperactivity are often expressed early on in life while, like the genetically based mood disorders, the edginess, anger, aggression, and impulsivity are triggered and show themselves, surface if you will, later chronologically, tending to be seen during the end of latency or early adolescence.

So, to my physician readers, particularly the non-psychiatrists, please consider the Prozac addition alternative. You'll be pleased with the results, as attested to by so many, many other doctors who have tried it already. It's doing the right thing for your patients.

To the parents who have children diagnosed with ADD/ADHD who had a good previous response to stimulant medication, discuss this very safe and minimally aggressive treatment alternative with your child's doctor before embarking on a more aggressive, extreme, or exotic polypharmacy treatment course.

Two brief but important therapy thoughts I'd like to share before I wind up this chapter:

First of all, I approach each and every one of my patients as special and unique. In a sense all the kids I've had the chance to work with over the last forty-plus years all dream of being unique, special, or extraordinary in one way or another, whether it be their goal to succeed in academics, sports, the arts, music, theater, etc. Once I have developed some level of a working relationship with them, I generally challenge them, specifically related to their particular and personal "dream"—that should they accomplish this goal in the future, they will have accomplished something truly "extraordinary."

When they agree that to be a superstar in the field they have dreamed about would, in fact, be unquestionably "extraordinary," I then break down the word itself. I point out that it's a compound word, actually made up of two words: extra and ordinary. So, my next question or challenge to them is, are they willing to do that something "extra," whatever it is, so they won't end up being just "ordinary"? Can they really walk the walk and not just talk the talk. This particular intervention is usually a wake-up call to most of my patients. I then explore with them specifically what extra really means in terms of personal sacrifice, commitment, and action so that someday they can truly be "extraordinary." In fact, in one way or another, from the very beginning of this writing with referral to the leaf and the dead fish, I challenge not just the kids, but all my readers—regardless of age, mental health professionals or not, nonparents and parents—go that extra mile, to do that something "extra" so that you won't end up being just "ordinary"! You can do it. I know you can do it, reach that distant goal with this understanding. Age is not a limiting factor! It's never too late to do or accomplish something "extraordinary." You just have to understand what "extra" means in your particular case.

Therapy thought number two revolves around the universal complaint of my young patients that their parents just don't get it, that mom and dad are so, so out of it, so old-fashioned, so behind the times, so passé, that they clearly have no idea, are without a clue, of what's really going on in today's world.

My initial response to this declaration is that I agree 100 percent with their analysis of the situation. This response on my part is usually somewhat disarming; their mind aligns me with their point of view but then allows me to question and challenge them to look at how selfish and narcissistic their stated position might actually be. Have they ever really invested even the smallest effort in terms of time and/or thought to try to understand what their parents' world is really like? What their parents might actually believe or feel emotionally? Usually this gambit therapeutically leads to intense discussion with positive perceptual and behavioral change on my patient's part. After all, their parents' teen years were actually decades ago.

My wife, partner for forty-six wonderful and fulfilling years of my life's highway, has often challenged me as to why I always basically "give away" all my therapeutic secrets, like the writing of this book, related to my success as a physician and psychiatrist. My answer has always simply been that, whether given credit or not, if any of my methods or recommendations has ever helped a single person, known or unknown to me, then my efforts have truly been worthwhile and more than fully rewarded. After all these years she finally understands this personal, professional philosophy of mine, that I just can't do it any other way. So, if you, my reader, have gleaned anything of value from this discussion that you can apply to yourself or someone that you truly care about, then I'm truly rewarded, even if I'll never know you or your life story.

We've now completed our journey together from birth through eighteen years of age. I hope that it has been informative and fun for you. It has been a joy for me to share with you some of what I have learned over time, some of my therapeutic "secrets," if you will, that have worked for me over these many years as a practicing psychiatrist. Hopefully, you'll understand yourself and others better, particularly the kids. If you've gained something, great! If this was simply an entertaining conversational read, that's fine too.

That's why I subtitled this work "Conversational Shrink Speak" in the first place. It was never my intention nor was it my hope to write a comprehensive or definitive work on psychiatry and human behavior, but only to share my thoughts and observations after forty years of practice, teaching and research, to try to express all this in common sense and easily understandable language as much as possible. I'll leave the comprehensive, definitive psychiatric work to the much bigger brains than mine!

If I have gotten just one of you to choose to swim against the current of life and not float passively like the dead fish out to the terminal sea, then I have accomplished a truly good thing. Please keep in mind my theory of faces and thought insertion. Remember that you can brainwash yourself in a positive way. But you've got to try, give it a real chance. You can do it! If you follow this aspect of Tsaoism, your life and destiny will be so much more under your own control and direction, and in addition to this you might be able to save a lot of money that would otherwise have been spent on therapy sessions!

Three addendums are added to the end of this work, as the material to be discussed in these additions is beyond my focus in the chapters on the first eighteen years. I hope you will enjoy these additions as well.

Addendum 1
Women, Men, and Blue Balls

As the end of the fairy tale goes: "And they lived happily ever after." Yeah right! Truth be known, as I have alluded to earlier and as if you didn't already know it, this "fantasy" only really happens in fairy tales. This addendum is what I like to think of as my "fools rush in where angels fear to tread" endeavor.

If you haven't already noticed, fairy tales or fantasies, probably by design and intention, don't document what happens in the "happily ever after," nor do they even make the slightest attempt to predict nor depict what the beautiful princess or handsome prince will look like as a direct result of the ravages of time as the years progress through the "ever after."

Years ago during one of his monologues, the stand-up comedian Jan Murray, while appearing on The Tonight Show with Johnny Carson, wondered where all the beautiful brides had gone. What happens to the beautiful princesses with their radiant smiles, sparkling eyes, and shapely figures? The obvious and clear-cut answer to Mr. Murray's question was that most, if not all, of those beautiful brides fell into the "black hole" of homemaking, working, one pregnancy or more, bearing a child or children, and raising those offspring. That'll take the sparkle out of your eye, the smile off your face, and the shape out of your figure! This is especially so if your prince turns out to actually be a toad, an all-too-common occurrence, and clearly related to his "toadhood" and his constant complaint about a lack of prince-transforming kisses, believes and behaves as if all of the negative consequences and the obligations of marriage are totally his wife's responsibility and fault.

I'll bet that many of you women have wished, although scientifically not by any stretch of the imagination realistically possible, that just for once, a man, any man, should carry a baby for nine months and experience the pain of childbirth! I obviously point this out, to some degree in the hope of increasing the awareness and sensitivity to this issue for men overall, although I accept that there is little chance of success for this to really ever happen. After all, future fathers usually are more selfishly concerned with and bummed out that the obstetrician/gynecologist has strongly recommended no sexual intercourse for the third trimester of their woman's pregnancy. Can you imagine? You have to go twelve weeks without getting "any"! I'll explain later why this is experienced as such a painful psychological and physical state for men overall. Guys, come on. If you think that's bad, it's just the beginning. Trust me! If you're the type who needs or feels entitled to almost constant "TLC" from your chosen woman or wife, disappointment is the order of the day.

With the arrival of the baby, you're definitely burnt toast! You are unquestionably second fiddle. The baby, and I emphasized why it should be this way in chapter 1, becomes the center of everything, the focus of almost all time and energy, leaving precious little time or energy for your wife to spend on you or your personal needs. Keep in mind that your wife also has little time to attend to her own personal needs, so try your best to be understanding and supportive. Here's a novel idea, guys: Why not be equally involved in the love and caring of the baby. After all, it's your baby too! Don't take the wife's lack of attention to you and your needs so personally. Remember crazy baby? If you happen to have skipped chapter 1, please go back and read it or read it again so that you can understand why it is so vitally important for "your" baby to be the center of everything.

Let's get back to looking at the oft-referred-to "battle of the sexes." A major problem is the experienced frustration with and the buildup over time of what I refer to as "emotional baggage." Remember my definition of anger being the perception or belief that you're not getting what you deserve? During the course of a longer-term relationship like marriage, little and big hurts happen continuously over the course of time. It is the nature of relationships unfortunately, but nonetheless a clear and ever present danger and reality.

Look at it in this way. Metaphorically speaking, life is like walking through an airport. You start out, as it is at the beginning of marriage, with little to no baggage, a song in your heart, and a bounce in your step. As you progress, each big hurt adds a new piece of luggage and unresolved angry feelings add weight to the bags you are already carrying. Eventually, you've gotten so many bags or they weigh so much that you just can't go on without the help of a skycap, aka "shrink," to ease and share your burden. This is one of the reasons why affairs, separations, or divorces occur with such frightening regularity. Think about it. It is so tempting to long for or go back to the no-baggage "spring in your step" feeling. But here's a thought that I hope may give you pause, and may even slow you down a bit before you take a decisive, no-turning-back course of action.

If you are capable of being open-minded and honest with yourself, truly not an easy thing to do, consider that without exception everyone comes into a new relationship with emotional baggage, obvious or hidden. That includes you and me! I cannot count the number of woman who, despite having exhausted every option possible in order to make a relationship work, have finally abandoned one relationship or marriage for another man only to realize they have just jumped out of the proverbial "frying pan into the fire." All too often I've heard the lament, "I thought he was totally different from my husband (or previous boyfriend) and he's really not." What did you expect? He's a man, isn't he?

Men experience similar frustrations, hurt, and anger, but, by nature, they will almost always identify the biggest and heaviest piece of baggage as not getting enough sex. Really? Can you imagine that? Now there's a statistical reality everyone already knows and accepts as true!

I'll never forget the scene in Woody Allen's movie *Love and Death* during which Diane Keaton's character, the much younger wife at the side of her significantly older husband's deathbed, laments, "We could've had sex more often," to which the dying elderly gentleman wistfully responds, "Once would've been nice."

Unfortunately, couples all too frequently don't talk to each other about the real issues that matter most to each of them in their relationship. Most women and men travel along the highway of life in parallel lanes while keeping their very personal thoughts, most intimate feelings, and emotional needs exclusively to themselves, continuing to keep much of their emotional baggage as a hidden personal burden, a sad, negative, and destructive state of affairs for most relationships.

Many professionals think that this conflict or "battle of the sexes" is because men and women don't speak the same language or don't come from the same planet. Being the contrarian that I tend to be, as if you haven't already figured that out by now, I disagree with that piece of conventional thinking or so-called wisdom. I believe it is more related to a lack of understanding about the different expectations and dreams of women and men and an almost universal lack of honest, open discussion.

In fact, it is the nature of dating that it be a deception. That's right, an out-and-out deception! Initially each party essentially presents themselves as "baggage free." It has to be this way. Let's put it this way: If you are honest enough, naive enough, or just plain stupid enough, you are not going to reveal all your hang-ups, problems, or "issues" during the first serious encounters with a potential significant other.

If the relationship, despite all odds, should progress to the big event, then I would like you to consider the meaning of "the wedding vows." Remember the part about "forsaking all others"? We're not talking about the generic all other women or men. Ladies, we are talking about giving up the diamond tiara of princesshood! Men, it's about relinquishing your role as "mommy's little man" forever. That's right, forever! That's why fathers tear up, as I did, when they walk down the aisle to officially hand over the love and caring of "daddy's" princess to another man. It is the same reason mothers sob quietly or not so quietly as "her" little man vows, "until death do us part," to devote all his love and commitment to that little blankity blank, uh, I mean, your now daughter-in-law and seals it with a kiss, a kiss for everyone to see! Guys, your mother sadly and nostalgically remembers at this point in the ceremony how you used to tell her ever so often that, "When I grow up, mommy, I'm going to marry you and take care of you." The tears flow from the emotional pain associated with this remembrance and loss.

The truth is I've never really thought that any man would be good enough for either one of my daughters. However, I eventually realized that it was really my own personal struggle with my separation and loss issues, and not the husbands Susan and Sam had chosen. I understood that it was actually more my problem! When I was able to get over my own emotionally driven issues and truly accept that it was the healthy and the "right" thing to do, to let them go physically and emotionally in order to start their own marriages and families, I was able to see my sons-in-law, Jay and J. L., as really good guys. Damn! Sometimes I wonder if it's such a good thing to be a psychiatrist, to realize that "forsaking all others" really meant me!

The problem here is that not all sons or daughters have a "shrink" for a parent, a parent who really understands what "forsaking all others" truly means. The number and prevalence of mother-in-law and father-in-law jokes clearly documents that in many or most instances there is always some family of origin stress or interference that can and usually does lead to discord and dysfunction in the marital relationship over time. The power of the family of origin dysfunction may foretell or be the major and primary reason or the destructive driving force underlying the ultimate failure of any given marriage.

Therefore, if you are already married or about to take the plunge, take a good honest look at your own family and your spouse's or future spouse's family to see if there is anything that may in any way significantly negatively impact your relationship further down the road. I know that's asking a lot. Doing this will go against the nature of what you are trying to accomplish: to win the approval of your future in-laws at almost any cost because you believe it's what will please your future spouse. Do it anyway! I'll bet dollars to doughnuts that if you really objectively look, you'll uncover something important that you can or can't do something about prior to tying the knot. You'll thank me later, I promise. At least you may be able to enter into this potentially lifetime commitment with your eyes partially open, keeping in mind the old adage that love is, after all, "blind."

You must always keep in mind that there should be and almost always remains present a deep and abiding emotional tie between daughters and their fathers and sons and their mothers. This bond, whether good or bad, will have a significant impact on any future developing marital relationship. My therapist wife would surely document at this point that at various times and to varying degrees during our marriage, having celebrated forty-six years together, that I have shouldered the role of husband, best friend, and father; and although at times it wasn't easy and was sometimes confusing to fulfill my wife's needs in each role, in the long run it has been a good and positive thing for the depth and longevity of our union. It really helped me to understand the different roles I had to play, and why I had to play them in order to make sure that our marital relationship would grow, mature, and work over time. However difficult as it was at times, the effort has proven to be truly worth it in the long term! She also certainly had to put up with me and my family, as well as play the many, I'm sure at times difficult, roles too.

Here's a hint for the guys. In an earlier chapter, I pointed out that when the more than 50 percent of American marriages end in divorce, the physical separation from their fathers significantly increases the number of emotionally damaged women as the judge or magistrate usually awards the physical custody of the children to the mother. I clarified earlier that symbolically, and in some ways in reality, the boys win the Oedipus struggle and get their mommies all for their own. On the other side of the coin, the girls lose. They will "lose" time spent with their father and the chance to experience and grow emotionally from that relationship in a normal healthy way. This means that depending on the girl's age and developmental stage at the time of the breakup, some level of emotional dysfunction will develop in the daughters of separation and divorce. The number and the intensity of the resultant emotional problems are usually inversely related to the chronological age of the daughter at the time of the breakup. This is not to imply that boys won't have just as many potential and deep emotional problems or hangups secondary to the over-determined relationship that evolves between a mother and son as the result of an absent father. This phenomenon is also observed with separations that may actually never end in divorce officially but are emotionally "de facto" divorces even if not legally or physically so.

How does this reality affect adult relationships? It means that statistically speaking well over half of all eligible women at any given point in time have experienced, to some degree or another, that their father, the relationship upon which all others will be judged in the future, wasn't there for them, that their daddy didn't really consistently love them, failed them repeatedly, and eventually rejected them or abandoned them emotionally and/or physically altogether! Similarly boys of marital breakups may have great difficulty, if not find it impossible, to break the emotional "apron strings" that tie them to their mothers.

The poisonous hidden baggage for women is the mentally formatted, negatively held belief that no matter how much they wish and long for "the happily ever after" scenario, there is in real time and real life no man so "perfect," fantasized or real, that it will ever actually happen for them in their lifetime. On the other hand, men will experience that they can never find a woman who's good enough to ever fulfill all their wants and needs like their mother did. And I'll bet their mothers will also continuously reinforce this belief, that there is in fact no woman, real or fictional, who understands and loves her "little man" the way mommy does!

For most women it starts out early in their dating experiences. So many of my young patients have sadly shared with me their sense of total desperation to hang on to their boyfriends at any cost, admitting they would do just about anything, sexual or otherwise, to hold on to their man! Eventually, as is the nature of dating early on, all these relationships end in another painful loss, leaving the young woman to believe she wasn't ever worthy or valued enough for her boyfriend to stay with her, causing a further lowering of her self-esteem and corruption of her self-face and self-image. Even worse from a psychological standpoint, this experience once again further reinforces and solidifies the belief that all relationships are doomed to eventually fail, always associated with another painful abandonment like the original and primary one experienced with her very own father. This experience leads to a common and destructive behavior pattern during young adult life for these women of separation and divorce that they sadly all too often exhibit. This internally fixated negative belief results in an observable behavior pattern in these women wherein their lives progress from and revolve around one histrionic "drama" to the next, potentially a vicious cycle that can become tragically lifelong in duration.

These women at their psychic core believe that if their current boyfriend or husband seems too good to be true, he probably is! They engage in behaviors that continuously "test" to see if he'll really stay in the relationship "no matter what." They'll constantly question his love and challenge his faithfulness and commitment. They'll openly make accusations that he'd rather hang out with his guy friends rather than spend time with her. She'll question and interrogate her man continuously about whether he looks at other women. Let's get real. All men look! It's the nature of men to look. The real deal is not to touch! She'll question his whereabouts or why he was a few minutes late here and there. She may even frankly accuse him of wanting to cheat on her or of actually cheating on her! All this behavior in a psychological sense is driven by a search for a father or father-like figure that she's never really experienced, and a deep belief as a result of this negative father experience that eventually every important man in her life will inevitably let her down and ultimately abandon her. Why should she feel otherwise, as in her lifetime, starting with her own father, this has historically been her experience over and over again?

As I have mentioned earlier, a father's love even in the best of circumstances for the most part can never really be revisited, reexperienced by any woman. A father adores and loves his daughter, supports and encourages her, would even die for her if called upon to do so. He'll do all this and have no expectation nor demand that his princess wash his clothes, cook his meals, or, God forbid, have sex with him! Yuck, that's incest. When I shared this with a professional friend of mine, he commented that the three expectations of men, although accurate as listed, were not in the order of priority; as far as men are concerned, sex always coming first. Point made!

Regardless of the order of priority, these three are generally the first things that a man, not inhibited like the woman's father by the taboo against incest, generally hopes for, wants, expects, or demands from his girlfriend or wife. Hey, guys, you can't compete nor do you want to compete with the "father thing." It truly presents a relational catch-22 for men. If you are involved with a woman who has had an essentially uninvolved, neglectful, hurtful, or absentee father, she will believe down deep that you really don't care about her feelings and will tend to continuously question your faithfulness and commitment to the relationship either covertly or quite openly, like searching through the pockets of your pants, your wallet, credit card records, cell phone records, such as saved numbers and text messages, or even saved computer information like e-mails.

The worse-case scenario here that I have already pointed out is when the woman actually unrelentingly pushes all your buttons and unconsciously or purposefully stretches the relationship to the breaking point just to see how much you can withstand or will take and still stay fully committed to her. This pushing away and testing of your limits gets old after awhile and eventually becomes a "self-fulfilling prophecy" when the man finally, in a state of angry exasperation and emotional fatigue, gives up and finally quits on the relationship, the result of his inability to tolerate or deal with any more "drama." Although everyone wants some excitement in a relationship, continuously high levels of drama and stress are like the red flags at the beach warning of an impending hurricane landfall or a potentially deadly undertow. Therefore, if you enter the water, or in this case make a final and complete commitment to the relationship with the red flags flying, you do so at your own risk and peril, the prudent course of action probably being not to get your feet wet in the first place! Unfortunately few men will heed or follow this warning, particularly if the woman in question is good-looking enough, "gorgeous," very closely resembling his idealized sexual image, behaves like the nymphomaniac of his fantasies, or presents as especially needy, which these particular women so often do and so many men find particularly and irresistibly attractive.

When the abandonment does finally happen as it inevitably will, of course the woman is hurt and feels devastated "one more time," but in an emotionally distorted sort of way she'll feel some comfort and sense of relief in that her suspicions were proven to be right and validated once again, that like her father and all the other men who have revolved through her life since, you never intended to really commit to her after all. Bummer! What a waste of time, effort, and emotion. Guys, be aware and make every effort to avoid this emotional trap relationship. Heed the red flags that are flying! Stay out of the water or you may drown!

If you're currently in a relationship like this that you think is really worth saving, then this is when I strongly recommend that couples try premarital or marital therapy as this may be a very helpful process to both parties involved, helping to clarify whether or not it is "reasonable" to go forward with the relationship in question. If it should become clear through the therapeutic work that there really is no future for this relationship, it can help both parties save significant time and emotional energy that would otherwise have been wasted on a psychologically lost cause. Hopefully, the counselor you find to work with the two of you on such issues understands and has experience with the material I've been discussing here. Otherwise, it may ultimately be a waste of your time, effort, and money.

For my women readers, if this is an experience that sounds uncomfortably familiar and repetitive to you, then I suggest that you consider getting professional help in order to break this negative, ultimately self-destructive, and emotionally painful personal cycle so that you will have some chance of eventually being able to participate in a positive, progressing, loving, and lasting adult relationship at some point in the future. It can be accomplished. After all, it's what you really want anyway, isn't it? I've been that "skycap shrink" who has helped many young women dump some of their heavier personal baggage and as a result change the direction and focus of their relationships, significantly decreasing the amount of "drama" in their lives and improving their chances of finding happiness.

Hopefully, reading this material has already helped a little. It is truly "a state of mind" that can be overcome and altered in a clearly positive, constructive, psychological way.

I mentioned that a friend pointed out that sex is the number one priority for men. No big surprise here, right? This being the reality, I have some advice for women. First of all, it's important to gain some real understanding of men and their "secret" sex lives. So, ladies, please read on if you really want to learn more about your men.

I have discussed earlier that men, as a general rule, during the preadolescent and early adolescent years are exposed to sexual material from all directions and media sources. They diligently study and input all the available information and format in the hard drive of their minds their ideal, sexual woman. For my generation it was Marilyn. Today's is Pamela or a Pamela look-alike. In fact it is my observation and professional belief that there exists in the collective minds of men, based on cultural standards and early exposure to sexually tagged material, an almost universally held idealized sexual woman image. If you think about it, Marilyn and Pamela do look an awful lot alike. Related to my theory of faces, it seems that there also exists an almost universally held ideal sexual face in the collective minds of men.

While standing in line recently waiting to be checked out at the supermarket, I was flipping through the pages of the latest automobile magazine when I turned the page to immediately be confronted by the picture of a model draped over a motorcycle. Most of the two-page spread was quite dark in nature, so the blond hair and the "face" of the model are what jumped out at me. At first I thought the model was Jessica Simpson. However, I learned that it was some new model/sex symbol, Marisa Miller. I think the motorcycle in the ad was a Harley-Davidson, but I'm not sure nor did I care as I'm not a cycle enthusiast. This experience and understanding the media mantra that "sex sells" further confirmed my belief that there exists a universal sexual "face" that is stimulus enough to elicit a sexual arousal response in most men regardless of the attached body. If you think about it, if you just did some very minor adjustments to the makeup and hair color or style of Marisa, Pamela, Jessica, Jenna, Angelina, Michelle, Bridgette, or Marilyn, their faces would be strikingly similar. This is further documented during televised sporting events when the cameramen pan the crowd during downtime in the action and always seem to find that "face" in the crowd. Most recently during the press conference of President-elect Obama related to his transition team, there was a face behind him and to the left that I'll bet piqued the interest of many if not all male viewers and distracted them from what Obama was saying! Of course, there will always be socio-cultural differences that come into play. Nice segue!

The other night I was channel surfing and came upon the Miss Universe Pageant. Having no interest in watching beautiful women parading around in various states of dress or undress, I was compelled to watch purely for scientific research reasons. Just kidding, but not really! The segment of the program that I had randomly stumbled upon was "the photo shoot." Keeping in mind that the contestants are supposed to be the most beautiful women in "the universe," talent is not a factor in the judging, so there was no baton twirling or trampoline acts to distract or bore the audience or judges.

I was struck as I watched that the science of genetic engineering or plastic surgery had finally reached a zenith. It was almost like watching science fiction rather than a beauty pageant. All the contestants looked like clones! I mean, if ten of the contestants were put in a police lineup, I wouldn't be able to tell them apart. They all had beautifully styled hair, big eyes, pert noses, sparkling white teeth, nary a snaggletooth in this group, and very full, pouty, sensuous sexy lips. This observation further documented what I have alluded to earlier and dovetailed very well with the face theory in that it occurred to me that, at least in the case of men, there does actually exist a mentally formatted sexually tagged face, in effect a face that literally "stands out" in a crowd and will then become the focus of almost all the male eyes present in any given situation, and will stimulate or precipitate some level of a sexual response or arousal in almost all the men present. If you think about it, guys, you've gone through this experience multiple times.

Beyond the commonality of their "faces," the contestants were all, each and every one, very sexy and overall very close to the universally held image in the minds of most men! Although there was some variation in hair color, the majority being various shades of blond, and some variation in the color of their big eyes, from the neck down they were all essentially identical twins. They all had thin shapely arms and shapely legs accentuated by very high heels. No cellulite or cottage cheese areas for these girls! Their tummies were softly cut, no bowl full of jelly here either, and their derrieres appeared round and firm. Without exception they all showed off their large, I'm sure surgically enhanced, breasts which stimulated the men in the audience and those watching on television around the world to recall warm and fond memories of breast-feeding and instinctively to experience a reflexive pucker response. I am only half kidding here! Each man knows this male reaction is true, whether or not he openly admits to it, that each and every man harbors somewhere in his mind such an irresistible female image and an associated fascination with women's breasts. This conclusion has been confirmed over and over again through my professional observation and understanding from tens of thousands of hours listening to the feelings and thoughts of so many young men. I've already explained the pre-literal emotional origins for this phenomenon in chapter 1. Related to this aspect of female sexuality, there are those who criticize "boob jobs" as being too big or too perky. I've already explained the size issue. The perky critique usually centers around the fact that augmented breasts appear too firm and/or the breast skin appears too taut. However, once again referring back to pregnancy, during the third trimester and through the nursing stage, this is the physical appearance and state of the woman's breast, too big and too perky. Therefore, this may explain why not many negative criticisms are forthcoming or really voiced despite the large number of augmentations.

This thought reminds me of an event that occurred about twenty years ago. It is also apropos that women should get a better grip on the "secret" sexual lives of their men.

In conjunction with an annual medical society meeting in Virginia, I was asked to speak to the medical wives' auxiliary. For whatever reason, the president of the auxiliary asked me to speak about the challenges to the relationship between men and women, specifically focused on the relationship that exists between physicians and their wives.

After an elegant lunch, accompanied by an excellent white wine, I began the requested talk. The part of my talk that drew the most interest, questions, and discussion was the elucidation of the internally formatted, irresistible, fantasized ideal sexual woman. My audience of wives was fascinated with this concept or idea but initially denied that, "My husband is anything like that." My initial internal thought, although appropriately not openly stated, was to wonder what planet these women had been living on anyway? It couldn't be planet Earth! However, suppressing the impulse to openly state such, I challenged the group of women to engage in a behavior that would either prove or disprove my "hypothesis." I challenged my audience to engage in some CSI work.

First, I had to lay the groundwork. I asked the ladies if their husbands still received or perused any "men's" magazines. Most of the wives responded that this was indeed so to a greater or lesser degree. Next I asked them if they were curious to really find out what each of their husband's fantasized ideal woman looked like. Some of the women jokingly responded that they probably didn't really want to know, but the majority present encouraged me to please continue.

My next step involved a minor violation of their husbands' privacy! The violation was for each wife to search through the husband's closet, desk, or any other private or secret storage space where he might sequester such "personal" material. If the wife found any such material, which she usually did if she searched diligently enough, then I suggested that she check the date of the uncovered evidence.

A number of the women, at this point, asked why the date was so important. I responded that it was a matter of human behavior, in this case the behavior of men in this situation in particular. I went on to explain that soft- to hard-core pornography is distributed continuously. I used Playboy as an example, to which a number of the wives responded that Playboy indeed was actually delivered to their homes every month, showing that Playboy had gained some level of societal respectability and acceptability, at least it would appear to be so as evidenced by its general acceptance by American women. This societal acceptance or respectability noted, I continued by pointing out that it was all a matter of "natural selection," in this case the survival of the sexiest!

Continuing to use Playboy as the example, I pointed out, as some of my audience had already reported, that it is published and distributed on a monthly basis, year after year. Therefore, every month their husbands, in the past and currently, would review the number of pictorials presented in that particular issue and experience some level of response—from no response at all to extreme arousal. The natural selection process plays out in the no to minimal arousal issue being discarded, abandoned if you will, or put away in storage should the individual physician have some pack rat tendencies. The "hot" or high arousal issue tends to stay close at hand, so to speak. It is only those issues that get a rise out of a man that he "naturally selects" to keep, and the others are forsaken. I pointed out that the chosen material found will in most instances be out of date because each man's fantasized perfect sexual woman has some unique physical characteristics that he personally started formatting in preadolescence and has continued to refine and enhance over the intervening years. This process having been explained, I advised that the wives look at the portrayed woman or women in the out-of-date issue or issues to learn what image sexually aroused and excited their husbands from a visual stimulus point of reference.

My presentation was well-received overall as evidenced by the lively and extensive question and answer period that followed. The impact of my talk was clearly documented as five of the participants called me at various times later on to tell me that, driven by irresistible curiosity of course, they had done their CSI homework and indeed found the predicted out-of-date material. They all said that although they were initially skeptical, they were surprised to find out that I was clearly correct in what I predicted they would find. Imagine that! All five of them were pleased to share with me confidentially that the uncovered images were quite similar to their own personal appearance.

One wife in particular, during the follow-up phone conversation, shared with me that she had always been painfully self-conscious of her naturally red hair, and over the years had tried dying it various different colors and shades. When she had followed my instruction, she discovered that her husband's fantasy women were all redheads! She felt wonderful about this revelation and finally understood why her husband openly questioned or rather strongly complained about why she spent so much time, effort, and money on changing her hair color. Here she thought it was all about spending too much money while all along it was about her husband's internalized ideal sexual woman!

I've sometimes wondered about the women who never did call me. I wonder what they might have found. I bet curiosity or the irresistible power of thought insertion got them to look. Maybe what they discovered was too disturbing to them to be shared, even with the one who inserted this apparently novel idea into their minds in the first place. Of course, they might have found nothing, although that's highly unlikely.

So here's one of the big challenges or problems for long-term relationships. As the particular man or any man ages through his teens, twenties, thirties, forties, fifties, sixties, seventies, and beyond, although he ages with each passing day, the idealized image basically doesn't age a day! That's right. It basically doesn't age a single day! Maybe because the image is formatted so early on and refined during the early developmental years, it doesn't significantly change or age over time, despite the aging of the man! When I have pointed this out to many of my own generation and even older men, the universal response has basically been, "Damn, you're absolutely right!" "I've never thought about it that way until you pointed it out. But you're spot-on about that." This truth obviously presents a real and significant challenge to the longevity of any relationship between a woman and a man, especially if the vast majority of the value of the relationship from the man's point of view is ascribed to the physical proximity of his wife or partner to his secretly held ideal sexual woman.

On the other hand, the brain of a woman clearly doesn't work the same way. Women don't seem to establish such a fixed, specific idealized sexual object. In fact, many of the young women I've worked with report that their ideal man is far from fixed and is actually quite fluid in nature depending on the girl's age and emotional development. For example, as I discussed in chapter 5, the "bad boys" or bad boy image will be seen as irresistibly cute early on. Later, as this "boy crazy" phase recedes, then the current pop entertainment figures and icons will take precedence, eventually morphing into personality characteristics like a sense of humor, steadiness of emotion, sensitivity, intelligence, success. Finally, women will usually find men with the closest approximation to the characteristics of the alpha males in our society as most appealing, this all evolving without a fixed, formatted ideal sexual man in a purely physical sense. This may be in some part related to being less driven by hormones or the anatomical, physiologic difference in the experience of orgasm. In any case it would appear that attraction or attractiveness is generally more emotionally based for women often having little or no sexual connotation and more physically based for men and always related to sex. The definition of "hot" is clearly so different for women and men. Hot for a woman is more related to,

"He's so cute" and "I'd like to spend some time with him and get to know him." Hot from the man's perspective is, "I have to get in her pants."

The vast majority of the young women I have worked with tell me that they don't experience orgasm associated with every sexual experience. In fact, when being totally honest, a good percentage of them admit that they have "never" experienced an orgasm at all! This is consistent with the previously published data on human sexual behavior documenting that up to 40 percent of American women never experience an orgasm during their entire lifetime. I suspect the worldwide percent is about the same. The same young women have further shared with me their observation that it's clearly obvious guys have an orgasm "every single time," as evidenced by the man's muscle contractions, uncontrollable seizure-like movements, and groans of orgasmic pleasure often associated with proclamations of their religious faith such as, "Oh God! Oh God! I'm cumming!"

When I have asked women whether they have experienced anything near what they have observed with their partners, the almost universal answer is "No way"! Therefore, in terms of the orgasmic experience related to conventional vaginal intercourse, the incidence and intensity are vastly different for each of the sexes. In fact, many of the young women have told me that it is from the observation of the male experience of orgasm that they have learned to "fake it," realizing intuitively or in real time that carrying on this charade is very important to their male counterpart's ego and to the more total fulfillment of the experience for "him." Come on, guys, you have to admit that it's important to believe that your amazingly wonderful penis and your unsurpassed technique as a lover drive a woman to orgasmic heaven every time! Yeah sure! Here's the sad truth that dispels this generally and widely held male "delusion." In fact, many women report that they fake orgasm the vast majority of the time, having a much more successful percentage of reaching orgasm when manipulating themselves. It would appear that women, related to this specific behavior, are really good actors. I suspect the men reading this will be greatly disappointed or may even deny that this phenomenon or reality even exists as many of my personal friends and professional colleagues have insisted, but men have to keep in mind that their women "fake it" because they care about your feelings and ultimately they want to please you. This female behavior is most often not driven by negative motives like a wish to deceive or to manipulate.

Speaking of manipulation, in the "battle of the sexes" men often accuse women of actually withholding sex as a weapon that they use continuously and effectively against them. Although there may be some truth to this allegation in certain circumstances, the reality in regard to women in general is that it is extremely difficult to nearly impossible to "make love" when a woman is hurt and angry related to a behavioral indiscretion or perceived verbal attack. Men, if you don't know by now that women are not quick to "kiss and make up" after a disagreement, then you just don't understand the psyche or feelings of women. Remember, as I've pointed out, that your over-all attractiveness is for the most part emotionally and personality based. Therefore, during and immediately following a disagreement or fight, despite being a most handsome stud, at least in your own mind, you're looking pretty damn ugly and totally unattractive to her emotionally at that particular moment in time.

I would be remiss not to point out the problem that most women experience with their first experience of sexual intercourse and how it impacts their overall and ongoing feelings about sexual intercourse and orgasm. During the course of treatment, many of my adolescent girls have reported that they had recently "lost" their virginity. In most cases they initially have tried to paint the picture of this event in the most positive of terms, that it was supposedly "great" or "wonderful." When I have then responded that they were exhibiting the "Pinocchio effect," as what they were saying just didn't make sense to me as a physician and couldn't possibly be true, without exception they all went on to confess that, as a first experience goes, it was really "awful."

From an anatomical and physiologic standpoint, this almost always has to be the truth. First of all, in most cases they've never inserted or had inserted an object the size of an erect male penis prior to this first experience. This in itself is painful enough from a purely physical perspective: big object, relatively small opening! How much fun was your first colonoscopy? Were you even awake for the procedure? Second, the natural lubrication process for most girls having not been in any way fully developed at this point in their lives adds further to the pain experienced. Can you imagine the insertion of the colonoscope without any lubricant? Third, the hymen or "maiden form" is torn and broken secondary to penetration with resultant bleeding. Fourth, the event is fraught with prohibition and religious or parental censure. Fifth, anxiety is extreme with the fear of discovery. Sixth, there is usually some level of remorse over loss of their virginity. Finally, whether or not protection is used, there is always some fear of pregnancy or of contracting an STD. And, speaking of protection, if a condom is not used, then the guy often spews ejaculate all over the place, the smell of which, accompanied by a mimicked gag reaction, was described by one of my more articulate and demonstrative young woman patients as smelling like "Clorox." You get the picture, right? The first sexual intercourse experience for a woman by its nature has to be painful, yucky, and emotionally troubling. Is it any wonder that women and men experience intercourse so differently, and therefore approach it and feel so differently about it! It's truly a wonder that any women, based on this first experience, ever go on to truly enjoy sexual intercourse or experience a true and fulfilling orgasm.

Guys, it behooves you to be more understanding. Could you imagine if your first very first sexual experience was associated with massive pain and your penis was bleeding when you were done? Not a pretty picture that you would even want to think about, is it?

One of the major focal points of the "battle" is in a physiologic sense neither party's fault. It's a matter of a significant misunderstanding. In the sexuality of men it all starts with the ascendency of sex hormones and the onset of the production of sperm, a robust ongoing and continuous process until the so-called "male menopause." Yeah, guys, as I've said previously, it happens to all of us eventually if we live long enough! Sorry! In any case, as the sperm is produced, it is stored in the vas deferens, in effect a small storage sack, until its release via ejaculation. However, ejaculate is not pure sperm—the actual volume of sperm amounting to less than half a drop—but is a mixture of sperm and fluids contributed mainly from the seminal vesicles, the Cowper's glands and prostate gland which alkaline fluids, remember the Clorox smell, are essential for the transport and survival of the sperm. If the vas deferens, seminal vesicles, Cowper's glands, and prostate don't release their stored contents on a regular basis, then their contents steadily increase in volume and stretch the walls of each storage entity.

Physiologically this is analogous to the storage of urine in another of the body's retention organs, the bladder. As the volume of urine in the bladder reaches toward maximum capacity, the bladder wall is stretched to the extreme, and as a result the sensory sympathetic and parasympathetic nerves of the pelvic plexus, triggered by this stretching event, convey a sense of discomfort and urgency that can reach the extreme and can be experienced as actual pain. Being able to finally urinate after reaching this extreme physiologic state is experienced as decreasing and ultimately eliminating all sense of tension, discomfort, or pain, actually a somewhat pleasurable experience, in effect a "mini" orgasm-like experience. Both women and men have this experience of simultaneous relief and pleasure or mini orgasm because it feels "so good" when you can finally relieve yourself. In fact, both women and men when they relieve themselves of an extremely full bladder condition often close their eyes and experience some involuntary muscle movement or twitches and mutter words like "Oh!" or "Ah!" because finally getting relief truly feels so good.

Related to this, I am reminded of the story of some tourists who came upon a monk squatting on the side of the road who was actively flagellating his back. When the tourists stopped and asked the monk why he was engaging in self-inflicted pain of such magnitude, he responded, "Because it feels so good when I stop." Thus is established the clear-cut relationship between the relief of tension or pain and the experience of pleasure. Therefore, it makes logical and scientific sense that the greater the pain, the greater the relief and the greater the resultant experience of pleasure. As already noted, we all have experienced how great or pleasurable it truly feels when we are able to "relieve" ourselves just before our bladders are about to burst. That's why men experience the greatest, most fulfilling orgasms when they ultimately find "relief" from their greatest levels of perceived sexual tension and pain. This also relates to why "mainlining" heroin is experienced as an orgasm-like experience, as the intravenous infusion of the opiate eliminates all perception of tension or pain.

In the case of men specifically, as the contents of the vas deferens, seminal vesicles, Cowper's glands, and prostate approach bursting levels due to delayed time between ejaculatory events or due to extreme or extended stimulation, men experience a progressive sense of tension and discomfort that at the extreme can actually be painful, a condition commonly referred to as "blue balls." However, this particular popularly held view is medically inaccurate and anatomically incorrect. The "blue" coloration is accurate as it is the result of "cyanosis," a naturally occurring phenomenon that exists when blood is prevented from recycling normally. For example, if you were to place a tight elastic tourniquet around your wrist that effectively restricted or totally stopped return blood flow from your hand, your fingers and particularly your nail beds would take on a distinctively bluish hue within a few minutes. From a physical anatomical standpoint this is exactly what happens when a man has an erection. In effect, secondary to a state of sexual arousal, the blood flow exiting the penis is blocked. It is the resultant trapped blood with nowhere to go that swells the penis, resulting in an erection or "boner," another misnomer here as there is no bone in a boner. In most circumstances relief through ejaculation releases the blockade of the outward flow of blood, and the man's penis quickly returns to its resting flaccid state.

However, should ejaculatory relief be delayed a significant amount of time, then the trapped non-recycled blood, as in the example of the band around the wrist, will start to demonstrate as the result of cyanosis a dusky bluish coloration. So, it's not the man's testicles or "balls" that turn blue, as he can't actually see them directly in any case; it's actually the head of his penis. So, the more accurate medical terminology to describe this physiologic state should be "blue head," but this scientific explanation is not intended to change the commonly held lexicon in American society. So, "blue balls" it is and should remain so.

It is exactly this condition that all the erectile dysfunction drugs so actively warn about: "Should you experience an erection lasting four hours or longer, seek immediate medical help." No kidding! Although guys would like to fantasize or believe that being really "hard" for four hours or more would be an "awesome" experience, it's really much closer to an "awful" experience. Consider the hand analogy. If a restriction to the blood flow to your hand occurred for four hours or more for whatever reason, and EMTs know from their training and experience that you must release tourniquet pressure intermittently in order to save a traumatized limb, one of the medical/surgical interventions that would have to be seriously considered without some pressure release would be to amputate the hand in question. That's right, amputate! So, although the state of "blue balls" or "priapism" may be desirable for shorter or reasonably moderate periods of time due to the enhancement of the male orgasm experience, its presence for any extended period of time really isn't an awesomely good thing nor a physiologic state to be in. Guys, you really don't want to know or experience the potential medical/surgical interventions that treat the extended presence of blue balls! It's scary. You don't want anything amputated, do you? As the saying goes, if you are going through an erectile event like this, "Be afraid. Be really afraid!" Get medical help immediately.

Anatomically, although women have ovaries, the equivalent of men's testicles, they don't have any equivalent to the male vas deferens, seminal vesicles, Cowper's glands, or prostate. They usually release just one ovum or egg per month versus the millions upon millions of sperm that a man continuously produces monthly. Therefore, although women can share from experience and understand the full bladder phenomenon, they cannot experientially comprehend the male blue balls experience because physically their reproductive anatomy is so different. They don't have any storage sacks or vesicles to swell up that would drive a sense of discomfort, urgency, or pain. So, not dissimilar to women wanting a man to experience pregnancy and childbirth, men would love for a woman to truly experience the frustration and pain that they experience without any sexual "relief." This physiologically and anatomically explains why there is such a discrepancy in the frequency and intensity of sexual drive or desire between women and men.

Just like having to urinate in order to "relieve" themselves, to a greater or lesser degree, men are driven to "relieve" themselves sexually on a regular basis, more frequently with youth, up to three or four times a day, and progressively less so with age. This physiologic need for relief is documented by the frequency of male masturbatory activity and the occurrence of "wet dreams" when masturbatory relief is not available secondary to physical or psychological constraints. This likely explains why women aren't driven to nor do they masturbate anywhere nearly as frequently as men and even more importantly why they don't experience orgasm as intensely and as pleasurably as men since they don't have the storage sacks that continuously fill and expand to an urgently painful state, exemplifying in this instance the truth, related to sex, of the saying, "No pain, no gain!"

The women I've worked with who do in fact masturbate with any frequency report that the desire to engage in such behavior is "driven" more by an emotional state of tension or frustration that is most often totally unrelated to actual sexuality or sex drive. Therefore, masturbation for women is more emotionally based with a lesser component of sexuality while for men the major component is relief of sexual tension with a lesser component being emotionality related. Hopefully after reading this information, women will have a greater understanding of what men go through and may, as a result of this insight, be more sympathetic just as they would like men to understand and be more sympathetic about the pain of pregnancy and childbirth. Similarly men should be more aware of and hold important the significant emotional component of a woman's sexuality. Based on this, "Cher Cher la Femme" for men is simultaneously driven by Cher Cher la "Relief." So, through this insight it is my hope that women can be more understanding and supportive of this real physiologic need of men and hopefully won't use this knowledge to serve more sinister motives or purposes.

I would truly be remiss if I didn't comment here that another major difference in the experience of sexual intercourse between women and men, particularly in the case of unprotected sex, is the transfer of DNA. In the case of the woman, she receives a large and rich source of genetic material in the form of sperm cells that is absorbed and incorporated into her own body, this happening in every instance when a particular man or when any man deposits semen in her vagina. There is some truth to the saying that when one engages in sexual intercourse, you are, in effect, having sex with all their previous partners. More precisely, every time a woman engages in unprotected sex, she absorbs and incorporates into her body that particular man's DNA. On the other hand, the man usually doesn't receive any genetic material from a woman during a sexual encounter. This explains the high incidence of the transmittal of the HIV virus from men to women and not vice versa. My women readers should really think about this. It may significantly change your thinking about engaging in unprotected sex! It should.

In terms of the masturbatory experience, as clarified earlier, there also exists a great disparity between the sexes based on the physiologic and anatomic differences with this psychological caveat. For men, masturbation is always associated with fantasy that often has a consistent and repetitive theme or themes, involving his particular ideal sexual object. This is the result of the individual man's preadolescent formatting of the idealized sexual woman and his idealized sexual liaison with her that has been repeated and reinforced countless times over a man's lifetime via masturbation or actual intercourse with a woman. Men often, or always, need an actual physical stimulus or prop such as a picture or video accompanying the physical act, an integral part of the total masturbatory experience for them. Women apparently don't require the presence of such a visual physical stimulus nor is their fantasized encounter generally fixated on a single mode of sexual activity in order to reach orgasm when and if it does occur.

Many years ago I was a member of a study team that, for public health reasons, studied the psychological makeup and health practices of "call girls," high-end prostitutes. The women who participated were guaranteed their privacy and anonymity. They were identified by number only. They were also guaranteed legal immunity.

The protocol included some brief psychological profiling which was accomplished by a team psychologist and me. However, since this was a public health study, the major focus was on the more important areas, such as what practices these women used to prevent sexually transmitted diseases, how often they had medical checkups, and what the checkups entailed.

This was so long ago that HIV wasn't a concern as at that time it didn't even exist. The end result of the study basically demonstrated that these high-end "professional" women, as would have been expected, took great precautions and were basically disease-free, a good result from a public health standpoint and good for their ongoing business enterprises.

From my perspective the most interesting information, apropos to this writing, was the women reported that their customers, or "Johns" as they were often referred to back then, had a rather limited number of fantasies and that the repeat customers tended to utilize the same fantasy over and over again with little variation. This experience more or less queued my early interest in and led to some degree to the formulation of the concept of the idealized sexual woman and the attached rather "fixed" sexual fantasy that has been more clearly defined over decades through my work with tens of thousands of young women and young men.

The fluid aspect of the sexual object is documented in that women often have reported, almost universally, that men look more attractive with some silver in their hair and character lines in their face. Thank God for this progressively evolving perception of male attractiveness, particularly as it applies to the population of aging men! So many women, young to old, say that they still see Sean Connery as a very "sexy man." They love his voice, that he takes good care of himself, that he is always well-dressed, that he's perceived as strong, steady, unflappable, and still "hot"! Come on now! No offense intended to Mr. Connery, but the guy is in his seventies and it's reported that he needs a cane to get around!

Here's the catch: Sean Connery is a strong father figure. His acting persona is strong, calm, steady, protective, knowledgeable, and wise. In his more recent films he doesn't even consummate the relationship with the female lead as he had done so often while playing James Bond. In some way, ladies, doesn't Sean Connery's silver-screen character describe or in some way or another mimic your father, father surrogate, or wished-for father? So, although you may say he's really "hot," you really don't want to make love to or have sex with someone with an emotional profile that is so close to that of your father. Remember the taboo against incest? But women do seek and enjoy an intimate non-sexual relationship with such a man. As a consequence of this, women truly enjoy and find fulfilling a quiet dinner for two. Men enjoy sex for two! Women want to share the emotionally close experience of a walk on the beach. Men want to share sex! Women want to share the emotional experience of a romantic movie. Men want to share more sex! Yada. Yada. Yada.

For women, a great deal of the fulfillment in a relationship is found in the sharing and overall closeness, this almost being an essential prerequisite for intercourse or orgasm to occur for them. For men, the end game is always orgasm or "relief," and the quality of the relationship may have little to no real meaning for them.

Remember what I explained about preadolescent and adolescent masturbatory fantasy and behavior? For boys, all fantasized interactions with their idealized woman climaxes in orgasm. So that becomes the expectation or wish for all their interactions with the real women in their lives. Boy, are they going to be disappointed as they grow up! I cannot count the number of my male teenage patients over the years who have reported that they are willing to put up with "so much shit" in the hope of getting into the girl's pants, with the ultimate result of seldom to never succeeding.

Armed with this knowledge and understanding, what is a woman supposed to do? Beyond just taking really good care of herself physically, I recommend and endorse investing in good cosmetics and using a competent hairstylist. I'm certainly not against the cosmetic effect and the value of Botox or the employ of a top-notch plastic surgeon if affordable. In addition to these plans of action, and if you don't happen to have the financial resources to pursue all the previous recommendations, you could talk to your man. Let me repeat: You could talk to your man! What a unique idea! Women are supposed to be the "communicators," right? So, communicate already! Earlier in this addendum I gave instruction as to how to uncover your man's fantasized ideal sexual woman, but I didn't tell you how to discover what he would like to do with her! That's the key. Remembering the experience of the call girls, each man has a rather fixed image born of masturbatory fantasizes and an almost equally fixed fantasized way he wants to have sex with that image! Now, he would secretly probably more than love to tell you and in this instance "share" what sexual acts or fantasies rock his world, but that can be far beyond too self-revealing and anxiety-producing psychologically. Men, for whatever reason or reasons, do seem to exhibit the so-called "Whore-Madonna complex" to a greater or lesser degree. How can they reveal to the mother of their children and their princess in the white gown whom they married before family and God their near lifelong, hidden sexual desires that could be and would most likely be perceived as dirty, perverted, or frankly sinful? They can't! This is especially so if the woman doesn't ask the right questions or never offers the opportunity for frank and open discussion, which is usually the case.

As a result of all this, men are unfortunately left to keep their secret sexual lives secret and to pursue their fantasies through other venues as documented by the millions of dollars spent annually on pornography, in strip clubs, and in legal or illegal houses of prostitution.

What fantasies are all of these men so driven to fulfill? What are they getting out of these activities that they are not getting fulfilled at home? As I have recommended previously that women should look around and find an out-of-date Playboy in order to discover her man's idealized sexual image, I would further recommend reading some of the stories or editorials. Can you believe it? There might actually be something to learn from the printed material beyond what catches the eye in the pictorials! Don't forget the material from chapter 5 about the adolescent male's relentless search for his "gorgeous nymphomaniac." The gorgeous part we now hopefully have a reasonably good handle on or understanding about; it's the nymphomaniac part that needs further clarification.

Therefore, look for audio/visual material like video tapes and DVDs or read the editorials. As in the case of the print material already discussed, men are once again so very predictable. Randomly exposed to all this material or purposefully seeking it out, they will once again characteristically cull out the material that doesn't clear their sexual excitement bar and discard such, only retaining those print and audio/visual items that rock their sexual boat!

If you cannot bring yourself to play CSI investigator, then think about what and why your man, and men in general, is spending his hard-earned money in the strip clubs of America. There are tens of thousands of strip clubs "from sea to shining sea." Why so many? It's simply a matter of Economics 101, "the law of supply and demand." If there wasn't such a great "demand," then there would be no reason to "supply" what is delivered in so many of these clubs on a nightly basis! Men, your men, are dropping their hard-earned money on the runways across America, in effect to pay for a group of young, sexy, scantily clad, perfumed women to rhythmically and seductively put their voluptuous breasts and crotches literally in their collective faces! To tease them! I'm sure you can find a much better use for all those dollars that are being so frivolously spent on such unnecessary, as you see it, activities.

Just as importantly, and in this instance probably "more" importantly, these women have on many different outfits that speak to various themes or "fantasies," basically something to engage and arouse each and every man's fantasy in the audience. The finale is of course getting down to the least coverage that the law will allow, very up close and personal.

For an even more intense experience that is more private and discreet, and for extra cash, the dancers offer "lap dances" to their more shy customers or those requiring or demanding less exposure to public eyes.

So, what's the real behavioral deal here? What is the lesson to be learned? Men don't go to strip clubs to get sexual intercourse! Again let me repeat: Men don't go to strip clubs to get laid! It's against the law. They go to the clubs to fulfill their need for sexual fantasy, and to live this fantasy out, over and over again, by showing the color of their money. They specifically pick or naturally "select" the dancer attired in the Playboy bunny costume, the cowgirl outfit, the cat woman, the nurse, the Daisy Duke, the French maid, the dominatrix. Each customer's fantasy gets played out and fulfilled in real time as his chosen dancer moves and strips "just for him"! After a few more drinks and a few more "fantasy" dances, the customer goes home feeling satisfied that he got his money's worth; and—to emphasize what I noted earlier—he didn't get any actual, real sex in terms of sexual intercourse. He didn't get laid. The irresistible impact of the power of the drive propelling this behavior is documented in the high level of repeat customer business and the financial success of such clubs from coast to coast.

How can this phenomenon possibly be explained? The only logical and realistic conclusion to be drawn from all this is that men like and want to be "teased"! Come on, guys, admit it. You know it's the truth. You like and need to be teased! That's why it has been called "striptease"!

Understanding the power and irresistibility of the male sexual fantasy helps to explain and identify the most dangerous women in

American society or any other society for that matter. These are the women who consciously or intuitively understand this sexual drive and need of men to be teased and ultimately to find relief—and by action or word imply that they are more than willing to "play" out his particular fantasy with him and offer the needed "relief" for his sexual pain. Whether the goal of these women is monetary, social, psychological, or otherwise, they represent a constant threat to the stability of all relationships within their sphere of interaction or influence. They are often very successful in seducing their targeted man, regardless of his marital or commitment status, if they can get into his head so to speak by tapping into his sexual fantasies or if they catch him at a time when his balls are particularly blue—the combination of which is a sexual perfect storm that is practically irresistible and potentially so very destructive. This combination of forces can crumble even the most virtuous of men. The power of the tease by itself can be seen in the ability of women who by their physical looks or appearance alone would not have been seen as a particularly effective seductresses, but in reality they are exactly that! These women, despite lacking some of the physical attributes associated with seduction, are particularly good at "mind games."

It then follows logically that the closer the physical approximation to the ideal sexual woman combined with the ability to tease or stimulate the man's sexual fantasy is an extremely powerful and irresistible combination, a combination that will engage and fixate the man on the particular woman in question and ramp up his drive, and focus the majority of his energy and efforts in order to consummate the relationship whether driven consciously or unconsciously.

How often have women with this "tease" mentality or seductive behaviors been able to severely disable or destroy what would otherwise have been a reasonably solid relationship between a woman and her husband? In fact, as noted before, all a given woman in this instance has to do is imply or say is that she is willing and wants to "play." The man in question will more often than not, given the chance, supply the fantasy from within his own mind, and unfortunately in most cases the game will be on.

An annual event that further documents the sexual fantasy needs of the American male psyche is that one night of the year when the strip clubs have essentially no business, besides the obvious Christmas time and Easter time. It is an evening during which inhibitions, conventional behavior, logic, and reality are all temporarily suspended. It's the night of trick or treat, witches and goblins: Halloween!

For whatever unknown reasons, wives, fiancées, and girlfriends acquiesce to their man's sexual fantasy and dress up or down, whichever the case may be, in costumes not dissimilar from those utilized by professional dancers and porn stars. The evening is usually accompanied by alcohol and other disinhibiting substances that heighten the aphrodisiac atmosphere. For this one night of the year so many women are willing to let go and let it "all hang out." And the men just love it! They get to live their fantasy, get teased, and at least have a chance to consummate their fantasy without being manhandled by a bouncer or arrested by the police. It would be interesting to find out if a study has been conducted to see if there is a statistically significant spike in the number of births nine months after the partying and fantasy role-playing of Halloween.

Unfortunately for men and their fantasy needs, there is generally no follow-up to this night of uninhibited debauchery and love-making. Standard operating procedure seems to be that the very next day the hot, sexy, fantasy outfit is relegated to the back of the closet, not to be seen for another 364 days! What a "bummer" from the male perspective. The men are then left to take on a great resemblance to the dying old man in Woody Allen's movie, basically saying to himself, "More than one night a year would be really nice."

So, ladies, assuming that you love your man despite all his flaws, failings, and faults, and truly want to hang on to him, why can't Halloween come more than once a year? It might inoculate your man against being an easy target for a designing woman who's willing and able to employ the tease.

The Halloween experience has given me an idea on how to elicit the male fantasy without having to engage in heavy and anxiety-producing conversation. The behavior of women on Halloween tells me that they are not really as innocent or naive as they generally pretend to be. In any case my suggestion here would be for the woman to express a genuine curiosity and willingness to go together to an "adult toy store." If your man agrees and you make the visit together, then just let him just randomly browse, and his sexual fantasy will be revealed without the need for detailed, anxiety-producing, intimate discussion or clarification. Besides you might see something that might pique your interest too!

Remember once again that men want and love the fantasy and the tease. If, for whatever reasons, you are unable or unwilling to address this well-established and clear-cut need, then I'm afraid that strip clubs, and all the other venues and outlets for pornography, soft and hardcore, will continue to do a really robust business, which may be fine by you. But surely of greater importance, your man will be that much more vulnerable to and an easier target for those dangerous women who are willing and able to engage in fantasy mind games and seduction.

This material reminds me of an experience that occurred several years ago and confirmed these observations of mine, particularly the power of a woman who in real life and real time so very closely approximates the formatted ideal sexual object. In this instance in regard to this particular woman, the tease factor was of little or no impact or importance overall.

I was doing a dinner talk several years ago at a very chic downtown restaurant that had just as chic a watering hole or bar on the premises. Being compulsively punctual, and in this case being quite early so as to evaluate the audio-visual setup and the size and acoustics of the room that I was going to be speaking in, I got to the venue a little over an hour early. The dinner crew wasn't quite ready, so I sat down at the bar and ordered a martini that I intended to nurse during the interlude while I passed the time. As it turned out, the bartender, in appearance, fulfilled almost all the parameters of the universal sexual woman for most men. I estimated that she was five foot eight. She had big, expressive blue eyes and a body fit to be a centerfold. Her hair was baby blond and pulled back into a French braid. She wore a red satin bustier that further enhanced her more than adequate bust size, and the rest of her outfit was tailored black silk slacks and heels. Now you may be wondering why I remember this bartender with such clarity and detail other than she was the closest thing to a real-time breathing fantasy. The answer is that I later learned that she had been nominated as one of the best-looking bartenders in America by Stuff magazine. This information made her particularly stand out in memory beyond her stunning good looks. It was also obvious that the judges, whoever they were, knew what they were doing! I was pretty sure the ability to mix drinks was a most important criteria to the judging process itself. Just kidding again! However, never being able to totally turn off my psychiatrist's mind completely, and, by training always and continuously studying human behavior, I was actually more struck by the customers and their behaviors.

The time was slightly after five thirty in the evening, and the patrons were all men, five at the bar seated to my left and nine or ten at tables in the bar area. She greeted all those who arrived with a warm, almost seductive smile and asked whether they wanted their "usual." When she delivered the drinks to the various tables in the bar area, all the male eyes tracked her every move. I suspect they were all undressing her in their minds' eyes.

As I sipped my drink, I eavesdropped on the conversations that were occurring in close proximity to me as best I could, without being obvious. The talk centered around or was to the effect that "Billie," was the highlight of their day. They further conversed that they attended happy hour here three times a week or even more frequently just to look at and fantasize about her. These were, at least by appearance, all very well-dressed and successful professional men of varying ages. From the conversations, I gathered that they were all lawyers, bankers, and stockbroker types. Two of the gentlemen sitting on the barstools directly to my left said, in effect, that if the stunning young blond woman would have either of them, they would leave their wives and children "in a heartbeat." In a heartbeat?! I just couldn't resist the opening and opportunity to comment.

Prefacing my question by noting that, of course, it was none of my business, I pointed out that their Billie might actually have a horrible personality and other hidden defects or flaws, like a ton of emotional baggage or even bad breath! Both businessmen responded, without a moment's hesitation, that even if everything I said was absolutely and undoubtedly true, it didn't really matter to either of them. "Man, just look at her!" Were these gentlemen really willing to give up their wives and children in exchange for this fantasy woman? What was missing at home that they were willing to invest so much time and money each week at this particular bar? Was she that overwhelmingly beautiful? Was this just a more acceptable tease experience in lieu of going to a strip club?

So what's the point of this story? Well, many of the patrons had other engagements and left, but not before paying the tab and leaving a tip. The smallest tip was ten dollars and the most was twenty dollars. The blond bartender had made well over one hundred dollars, or as they say in the business, "made bank," in less than an hour's work! And she didn't even have to strip or dance! She didn't have to tease at all. Her close physical approximation to what I believe to be the universally held ideal sexual woman in terms of the face and the accompanying body was the stimulus that elicited the individual and personal sexual fantasy response in each and every one of her male customers, and this reaction was what kept them coming back time and time again.

This scenario also reminded me of what a good friend and owner of a number of high-end restaurants and bars had explained to me in the past, that having beautiful sexy hostesses and bartenders are essential for business because they attract the men with money, the alpha males. This further documented the power of the tease, the thought insertion phenomenon, and its universal application to male behavior and economics.

These facts point to the concept that I believe to be true, that there exist women who so closely resemble the universally held, idealized sexual image of most men that these particular women, like Billie, don't even need to flirt or tease to trigger the sexual fantasies of most men. Just their physical appearance will be more than enough of a stimulus to precipitate all kinds of male erotic fantasies that may have no basis in the real world or in real time. Billie could have been as frigid as the South Pole in July as far as I know, but because of her appearance it really didn't matter to her customers or, more universally, to men in general.

It is, therefore, a terrible observation and conclusion, but it has become clearly evident to me over my years as a psychiatrist that fairly or unfairly the most important asset for a woman to have in American society today is to be good looking. There are, in fact, published psychiatric studies that support this conclusion that attractive women tend to get more intensive and better psychiatric/

psychological care than their less attractive counterparts. Movies like Cherry 2000 and The Stepford Wives further document the fantasies of men and their continuous and lifelong obsessive drive to obtain them.

So, to my women readers, you now know how to identify your husband's or a man's ideal sexual woman. You have some hint of what he would like to do with her now, but the most effective way to really know the truth is probably to ask. If you do, it can potentially lead to a closer, more enjoyable, more intimate, and more fulfilling relationship for both of you. Of course, you can choose to do nothing with what you have learned here and perpetuate the status quo. I understand the psychological reason for holding to this position. Just like men have a resistance secondary to wanting to keep their wives up on the virtuous pedestal, equally so women don't want to sully their view of their man. Nonetheless, the conspiracy of silence means more work for marital therapists and shrinks in general!

A perfect example of this took place a number of years ago. Within four weeks of my presentation at an international conference on mental health, I received a phone call from a multimillionaire industrialist. Somehow he had managed to be in the audience during my presentation. He was a gentleman in his early sixties and was in excellent physical health. During our initial phone conversation he stated that after hearing my talk he became convinced that I was the one psychiatrist who could help him. He noted that money was no object, and we eventually mutually agreed that I would reserve a Saturday for him and his wife.

The evening before the scheduled Saturday appointment, he and his wife arrived at the local airport in his corporate jet. They stayed that night at the finest oceanfront hotel and arrived at my office promptly at 9 a.m. on Saturday.

Frank asked Phyllis (both fictitious names) to wait in the lobby while he spoke to me privately first. Once we were alone, Frank shared with me that he and Phyllis had a wonderful marriage that had spanned almost forty years. They had three grown children whom they both loved very much and were blessed with five grandchildren whom they loved even more. As he had been lucky and extremely successful in business, they had more money than they could ever imagine spending, having residences in Atlanta, Monte

Carlo, and the Caribbean. It all sounded so positive and wonderful that I was initially at a loss to understand why in the world they were coming to see me.

Finally, after documenting how wonderfully their marriage had progressed over many years, Frank got down to his personal problem that predated his ever having met Phyllis and had been troubling him for many years.

He chronicled that it all started when he was a youngster growing up in one of the boroughs of New York City. When he was about twelve years old, he was walking home from school when his eye caught a glimpse of a magazine on top of some trash that was curbside waiting to be picked up. His attention was captured because the breeze was gently turning some of the pages back and forth. When he approached the trash heap, he clearly saw that the breeze-disturbed magazine was pornographic in nature. Since his family was of strong religious background, belief, and practice, he was initially in considerable conflict as to whether to ignore the flapping magazine or take possession of it. Driven by irresistible curiosity and the rising sexuality of early adolescence, he quickly chose the latter course of action. When he was sure that nobody was looking, he quickly sequestered the magazine in his backpack.

When he finally got home, he told his waiting mother that he had a lot of homework to do and that he was going right up to his room to get to work on it. He didn't tell his mother what he was really going to be working on! Once in the privacy of his bedroom, he anxiously and excitedly removed the forbidden magazine from his backpack.

Putting this experience in developmental perspective, little Frank was in the early phase of his developing male sexuality. His sexual curiosity and drive were clearly on the ascendancy, secondary to rising sex hormones, but his idealized sexual woman was far from being fully formatted, and he had no real idea of what he would like do to her or with her. What little Frank was about to be exposed to would be his first intense, sexually arousing thought insertion experience. What Frank saw on the pages of the porn magazine were images of women and men engaged in sado-masochistic sexual acts! Naturally, he was aroused by the sexually explicit pictures and further aroused by the accompanying text. This stimulus-response situation led to many repeatedly fulfilling and reinforcing orgasmic masturbatory experiences for him. This repetitious stimulus, pleasurable response experience solidified in Frank's psyche the primacy of "S&M" in reaching the ultimate sexually fulfilling experience. This is not to say, from a historical standpoint, that he didn't reach orgasm when fantasizing about or engaging in "straight" sex during his adolescence and early adult years. However, no matter how hard he tried, he was never able to replace S&M as his personally most arousing and fulfilling orgasmic sexual experience. He reported, with considerable guilt, that in order to increase his level of sexual excitement and pleasure, he often fantasized that he and his wife were engaged in various S&M behaviors while Phyllis had no idea what he was really thinking during the act of making love.

His personal discomfort was founded in his strict upbringing and the perceived societal standard against such behavior. So, for the many years of his marriage and business life, his driven fascination with S&M was well hidden from all concerned in his day-to-day life. He told me that on multiple occasions in the past and for periods of time up to as long as six months he had attempted to suppress the thoughts, drive, and behaviors. Behaviors? Yes, behaviors!

During most of the years of his marriage, he had employed the services of call girls to fulfill this driven part of his private sexuality. He hired these women to engage with him to play out different S&M fantasies. They would generally play the role of the dominatrix, and he was the dominated one or "slave," the roles originally depicted in the magazine. Although there was restraint and punishment in the fantasy enactments, the whips were faux and there was no real or significant pain meted out.

As the years went by, Frank experienced increasing levels of anxiety that his self-perceived "perverted secret" would come to light and he would lose the love and respect of Phyllis and his children and grandchildren. Interestingly, he wasn't particularly concerned about his business colleagues' reaction to such a discovery as he was sure they too engaged in not too dissimilar kinds of behaviors themselves.

After intently listening to Frank's story, I spent considerable time explaining to him the process of developing human sexuality, thought insertion, the staying power of first experiences, and the unchangeable aspects of formatted internal images and fantasies and their ongoing influence on human behavior—in this case his particular behavior.

At this point in the session, the question Frank appropriately asked was, based on what he had told me and what I had clarified for him, whether his situation was, in fact, "hopeless." I responded that in his case and at his age it was highly unlikely that the primacy of S&M could be significantly changed or the behavior permanently extinguished. However, I continued by clarifying that from what he had told me, he very much loved Phyllis and had experienced a generally satisfying sex life with her for many years, he had no real interest in being with another woman, and the only missing piece of their total sexual relationship as far as he was concerned was the S&M piece to the puzzle. Frank agreed with this analysis.

The next step was to explore and understand why he felt so much guilt and anxiety. Together we were able to determine that these feeling were based on his very structured, strict upbringing and familial religious beliefs. He was also influenced by his education.

Frank had completed a master's degree in business administration. During his undergraduate studies he took a number of psychology classes, and like so many students before and after him, Frank felt a great deal of the material applied "directly" to him personally. In particular he recalled that in his Abnormal Psychology textbook, in the section on human sexuality, his particular behavior was classified under "Deviations." This labeling of his preferred, although not exclusive, sexual behavior troubled him quite a bit back then and over the years following. I countered by pointing out that, by his own account, S&M was indeed "not exclusive" and that it had not reached a level of intensity that it had caused any significant damage to his marriage, family, or business enterprises. The damage, to whatever degree he experienced anxiety and guilt, was more internal and emotionally based, more to his internal self-face and self-esteem.

The solution for Frank was to find some way to significantly decrease or extinguish this anxiety and guilt. Frank admitted that what he had already learned in the first two hours of our session had helped in terms of his greater insight, understanding, and acceptance of what happened to him in preadolescence and its lasting impact on his psyche and sexual behavior. In fact, he reported he had already experienced some degree of "real" personal emotional relief. He seemed ready for the next step.

My next recommendation was that Phyllis should be involved in the therapeutic process. Frank's initial response to this suggestion was, not unexpectedly, negative. However, after a great deal of further discussion with a particular focus on the general, overall long-term honesty and strength in their marital relationship and Phyllis's good, supportive response to a number of negative life events or crises that had historically happened during their journey together, Frank saw the wisdom of my plan and its potential for real gain, and relented on his initial negative position. By this juncture in our work it was almost lunchtime, so we agreed that it would be appropriate to take a break. We planned to start the afternoon session by including Phyllis in the proceedings.

When we resumed a little after one thirty, Phyllis was, to say the least, very curious about what we could have been talking about for almost three hours that morning. I initiated the discussion by synopsizing the longevity and strength of their marital relationship, recalling some of the most difficult and challenging times that they had overcome "together." I emphasized that the difficult times had actually brought them closer together in the long term and had significantly strengthened and enriched the totality of their relationship. As you can see, I engaged in a lot of positive thought insertion as I laid the groundwork for the real task at hand. She agreed with all my observations. I concluded that what Frank was about to reveal would actually be less challenging than many of the events that had challenged the strength of their relational bond in the past, and it would potentially offer them an opportunity for even further closeness and relational fulfillment. I then invited Frank to share his "secret."

Hesitantly, Frank shared about his long-hidden sexual life. Phyllis's initial response was shock, some level of disbelief, anger, and revulsion. Frank cringed emotionally and to some degree physically at Phyllis's initial negative emotional reaction.

On the other hand, I was prepared for this initial negative response. By employing various therapeutic maneuvers, I was able to settle Phyllis down. One ploy, beyond my initial observation of what a long and strong marital relationship they had experienced together, was to point out that after all these years of marriage, she had to, at least intuitively if not actually, have known or felt that Frank was holding something back, that something was indeed missing. As a result of this intervention causing her to shoulder some of the responsibility, Phyllis did agree that, although she was not a suspicious person by nature, there were times over the years when she felt something was amiss. In fact, she admitted, with some small amount of guilt, that there were a few occasions when she worried there might be "another woman," but she never discovered any evidence to corroborate her anxiety or suspicions. Besides, she noted that she truly knew that Frank loved her and down deep was not a womanizer and was, quite to the contrary, a shy and very private person.

To make a longer story short, Phyllis was eventually intrigued and challenged by the situation presented to her, and at the end of two more hours of intense discussion they left my office, both of them saying that they were, despite being a little shaken by the process of this revelation, determined and committed to making it work out for the best.

Almost three years later I ran into Phyllis while vacationing in the Virgin Islands. She appeared happily surprised to see me, and she couldn't wait to tell me how wonderfully everything had eventually worked out. She reported that she felt "empowered" and so much closer to her husband now that they both shared and participated in his "secret." She was obviously very happy with the result of the intervention I had done with them a few years earlier.

The moral of this story is to emphasize the power and impact of our earliest experiences, pre-literal or literal. What if Frank's early formatting experience was exposure to child pornography? The psychological and behavioral fallout would clearly be more devastating personally for Frank based on his strong family religious values, and the acting out of his sexual fantasies would have rendered him a clear danger to society and its children! Therefore, you can see once again why I cannot emphasize strongly enough the need for the total eradication of any and all sources of child pornography.

The other value to be gleaned from this clinical vignette is that although Phyllis could not compete with the ageless formatted sexual woman of Frank's creation due to the realities of aging, she was perfectly able to compete with and engage in "the fantasy" of what Frank would like to do with his idealized sexual woman.

All the aforementioned material explains to a great degree the high percentage of infidelity in the relationships of women and men. Remember, it's the belief that we're not getting what we deserve out of the relationship that increases anger and, as a result, decreases the resistance to negative acting out. Since the end result for men is organism in any intimate interaction with a woman, then it's easy to see why men will engage in a random sexual affair with a stranger or a prostitute at a place like the Bunny Ranch in Nevada if the circumstances seem right, the woman resembles to some degree his idealized sexual woman, and he perceives that the woman is coming on to him, teasing him, or is actually getting paid to act out his particular personal sexual fantasy, the color of his balls also being a significant factor.

For women, since sexual intimacy has as one of its major goals being a commitment to a relationship at some level of intensity and a sharing of life's experiences together, they are less likely to have a random sexual encounter with a stranger as there can be no resultant commitment or any real potential to share life together. Affairs, when they do occur for women, generally involve some "fantasy" on the woman's part that there will eventually be some longer-term commitment to the relationship by her lover.

The relational aspect of sexual intimacy having more value than orgasm in women is further supported by the small percentage of women that actually experience an organism as a result of intercourse with a man. I have referred to this earlier. Since men basically experience orgasm 100 percent of the time and women don't, you can see that the motivation for the different sexes is clearly very disparate.

Another area of conflict for women and men is what usually happens immediately following the man's sexual relief. Nothing! That's right, basically "nothing" as far as the woman is concerned. Just like when a man has to pee, his sole focus and almost all of his energy is spent on finding an available toilet or urinal as soon as possible. Once he's "relieved," the previously sought, highly valued, and absolutely needed ceramic receptacle has no further value, real or emotional, and is immediately dropped from consciousness until the need to urinate raises its ugly head once again. This is not to imply that men see women and their vaginas as being similar to toilets, but it does explain why immediately after orgasm men generally go to sleep or turn on "the game."

Remember what I said about sex being all about orgasm for men and not so for women. So when the "sex game" is over for the man, the "football game" comes on. Wake up, guys! Remember it's all about emotion for your woman. How about a little quid pro quo, you know, this for that. Remember that your woman, despite what you may delusionally believe about your irresistibility and sexual prowess, does not feel or experience any great pressure or pain driving her to find "relief," nor does she experience an orgasm to anywhere near the intensity of pleasure that you experience, if she has one at all. So what does a woman get out of the experience? What does she really want? She wants and seeks emotional closeness. So going to sleep or turning on the football game just doesn't cut it! Spend some time with her after you've gotten off. Hold her close. Kiss her. Whisper sweet nothings into her ear, like how beautiful she is or still is. Tell her how much you really love her. Now we're talking about a total sexual experience that's fulfilling for both of you!

At this juncture, and in the interest of comic relief, I would like to offer a defense for us poor, innocent guys, at least in this one particular instance. One of the major battlegrounds for men and women other than the one that rages on over sex is how we tend to dress, how we coordinate our clothes, and the "unbelievable" color choices or combinations we come up with. A typical encounter between a man and a woman goes more or less like the following.

It's Saturday evening, and my wife and I have been invited out to dinner. We're getting ready to go, and I choose a black blazer, unbeknownst to me at the time that it's actually navy blue, light tan slacks, a black silk-blend mock turtleneck, medium brown slip-on shoes, and what I believe to be matching black socks, not unlike how I was convinced the blazer was black. Feeling pleased overall with how I look after a quick check in the mirror, I head down the stairs to leave for dinner with my wife. As I descend the stairs, my wife's steely gaze freezes me in mid step, halfway down the staircase. You guys know what I mean by "the gaze." She rolls her beautiful green eyes with distain, and I know I am in big trouble!

"You're not really going to wear that blazer out tonight are you?" I think to myself, Yeah, I was, but not anymore, I guess.

"I can't believe you didn't pick the black one." Gosh, I actually thought I had picked the black one! But, here's the problem. In my closet, which is illuminated by one of those sixty-watt energy-saving bulbs, hang two identical designer blazers, one black and the other navy blue. It's difficult, if not impossible, for me to differentiate between the two of them except in broad daylight, much less to the illumination of a sixty-watt energy-saving bulb. I really thought I had chosen the black one! Honest!

Here are the scientific facts in defense of us much-beleaguered men. Total color blindness, although the genetic code is transmitted through women—thank you, ladies—effects men over twenty times more frequently than women. If you then throw in some difficulty or deficit in the ability to discriminate shades of color like blues, greens, and yellows, then the odds increase to over 100-to-1 against the men! Ladies, think about it. Consider that your man, although I know you don't want to believe this, could be in that very large group of men who just cannot discriminate color or shades thereof. Over the years he has adapted to this handicap, if you will, and has gotten by basically seeing various shades of gray at worst and limited shades of color, like blue, green, and yellow at best.

Please consider this reality. This is what he's seen all his life! This is normal for him! He's actually clueless, unless he's been tested for color blindness and proven not to be so. This explains why when a woman asks her man to get the green-labeled bottle of extra virgin olive oil from the cupboard, when he with all good intentions actually goes to the cupboard to look for said green bottle, all the bottles appear to be various shades of gray. That's why men fail to find things that are "right under your nose" quite often or dress the way they do. With a very rare possible exception, we men really don't do these things to "piss off" our women! I would suggest the following for my women readers to consider.

Instead of rolling your beautiful eyes, presenting a thoroughly disgusted countenance, uttering in a negative, angry, or frustrated tone of voice that implies either directly or indirectly that we are incompetent or "stupid," remember the old saying that you catch more flies with honey than with vinegar.

For example, in my particular case, my wife could have nicely and helpfully commented, "Honey, I think that the other blazer would look so much better on you, and you probably should change the socks too." The end result in terms of my attire for the evening would have been the same in both instances. I would have changed the blazer and socks in either scenario. With the positive approach, we both end up enjoying the evening together. With the negative approach, there remains some level of tension, and as a result, a little extra weight is added to my personal emotional baggage as it relates to my wife.

After just defending the guys, I'm obligated to change direction somewhat in order to defend a particular identified group of women, the "gold diggers," the idea having been promulgated that these young women use their looks and/or sex to "land" rich older men, in effect going fishing for a "sugar daddy." I believe that it is in actuality the other way around, the exact opposite, and always has been. It has been my observation and experience that it is the older "alpha" males who are constantly seeking out the hottest new Barbie to debut on the social scene. Sadly, these beautiful young women, all of whom generally appear to have been produced from the same mold as previously explained, are just one more of the alpha male's "trophy" things, this being of little comfort to the spurned ex-wife. The new hot "thing", and I use the word thing purposely, is really no different from his Ferrari, yacht, private jet, or other badges of power, influence, and wealth. She's the trophy date and may ultimately become the next "trophy wife"!

Often, I jokingly comment to my wife when we are having dinner at a restaurant that is frequented by the local rich and famous, the place to be seen, if you will, that it's really nice to see how many "dads" are taking their "daughters" out to dinner this evening. She always responds, "Oh, stop being a psychiatrist all the time! And don't stare. You'll embarrass me." I don't believe that these young women are with older men because the men are really sexual studs, although I'll bet a number of them would like to think so. Sorry, guys! I also don't think that it's all about the man's money either, although I'm sure the money doesn't hurt and is part of the equation of power. In my opinion, what they're really attracted to is the aura of power, a chance to experience the circle of the so-called "movers and shakers," to be fawned over and taken care of even better than when they were "daddy's little princess." These beautiful young women more easily fall victim to this particular situation if their relationship with their own father was significantly lacking or dysfunctional. I don't believe it ultimately was their goal or scheme to replace the previous wife, as it turns out is often the case. It all goes back to Darwin and the Bunny Nation. The alpha male buck bunny gets to have his way with the most attractive doe bunnies. So, don't blame the pretty young "things" because it always has been and will remain the man's behavior and responsibility totally! It all goes back to the indelibly imprinted ideal sexual image not aging a day.

Based on understanding all that I have discussed concerning human behavior, men are clearly challenged and obligated to make a conscious effort to rise above their biological sexual urges and psychologically formatted behaviors to find, appreciate, and value a long-term relationship with a woman on many different levels and from many different perspectives, or maybe not, depending on where the particular man places his personal values.

Otherwise, we men will just be caving in to our instinctively driven mammalian behaviors. Are we men or are we rabbits? And I won't accept any quibbling about loving carrots or how carrots are good for your eyesight! Of course, with what my women readers have hopefully learned, they also are not without considerable responsibility as to what they contribute that is predictive to the longevity and quality of the relationship.

Happily married older couples that I've known have shared multiple things together far beyond the sexual relationship that tends to decrease in intensity over time. Some have shared a business or career goal. Others have shared a religious faith, a love of sports, gardening, literature, music or the arts, a love of life. They have shared and valued the raising of their children, and, if they're lucky, are involved in the raising of their grandchildren. They have shared the good times and the bad, the laughter and the tears, the totality of life's experience.

When I see in the media that Mr. and Mrs. Smith or some other married couple is celebrating their fiftieth wedding anniversary, I often wonder whether they were really happy for all those many years, or over time did they actually drift further and further apart emotionally, just staying together for religious, family, or other reasons. In this particular instance, it has always been the journey, the highway of life, that truly counts and not the ultimate and "terminal" destination. It's the quality of the fifty years and not getting to fifty years. A man has to weigh this, using all of the things I've mentioned already, against the never-ending pursuit of the ideal sexual woman. So many times I've heard and actually have seen that the second wife is a younger version of the first, and that the third is a younger version of the second! I would ask men, when sorely tempted, to apply the golden rule of "Do unto others as you would have them do unto you." Would you want your wife to be unfaithful to you? Think about it for a moment. Is there any meaningful value in true virtue?

Ladies, remember that you are not just helpless victims in all of this. Although I have strongly recommended that you should take good care of yourself, time and the inevitable process of aging will erode your ability to match or compete with the appearance of your man's ageless ideal sexual object because that image has been digitally enhanced and surgically improved and basically never ages a day. However, you can, if you explore or have the courage to ask what your man's fantasized sexual activity with that internal idealized image is, you can establish intimate common ground at least in that area of the relationship, which potentially can and will be fulfilling for both of you. You can and will feel truly empowered. Remember Frank and Phyllis?

Both a woman and a man engaged in any type of long-term meaningful relationship must hold dear those things in the relationship far beyond your personal emotional needs and strive to identify and fulfill those things that are equally meaningful to both of you.

Once you get past the frills and the cosmetic issues of the relationship, what is really important to understand? When you get down to basics, what is really at the core of it all? First, you have to look at false perception and doctrine held to be true by most adults, beliefs as to what constitutes a healthy adult relationship. In my many discussions on this subject which have taken place around the country with everyday regular people and professionals alike, they all basically took on a strong resemblance to bobble-head dolls with their heads shaking up and down affirming the notion that at the core of a good adult relationship there should be a 50/50 give and take between the two partners. Admit it! Your head nodded in the affirmative when I noted this belief. Welcome to the majority of believers.

In other words, it is generally held to be true that good healthy adult relationships should be sort of a 50/50 thing, a quid pro quo, a this-for-that equation, a give-and-take kind of thing. One person in the relationship should do such and such for the other person, and in return the recipient should reciprocate in kind. Every person or group that I've discussed this with understands and agrees with this principle. It is considered and held to be a universal and self-evident truth. You would in all likelihood agree. Right? Wrong! This universally held "delusion"—that's right, a delusion being a fixed belief that is clearly contradicted by object reality—just doesn't make common sense or any sense for that matter. Basically if all adults understand, ascribe to, and practice this inside-the-box concept of relationships, then how do you explain the greater than 50 percent divorce rate and so, so many more painfully failed relationships? The only logical, reasonable, and scientific answer, based on reality and the numbers, is that the give-and-take thing is flat-out wrong! It just doesn't work. It never has worked and it never will. It's just a delusion!

So how should adults relate, you ask? The answer has always been and still is alive and well right in front of us. We just haven't taken the time or made the effort to look at it. It's easier to hold on to old beliefs and not rock the boat. What is it then if what has been held to be true isn't? It's the relationship that exists between a parent and a child. That's the answer. Parents love their child with all their heart and being. They willingly will expend the majority of their thought and energy to protect, encourage, and raise their child. Should the occasion arise, they would even make the ultimate sacrifice of giving up their life in order to spare their child's life. This is no 50/50, quid quo pro relationship, not even close. The giving is practically 100 percent on the parent's part.

How often have we seen on the news, through the Internet,

or read newspaper accounts where after natural disasters or the devastation of civil war when humanitarian aid finally reaches the displaced and starving people, when aid workers are finally able to distribute bread to the starving masses, a terribly hungry and starving mother or father, after waiting patiently for hours in often harsh conditions, will gratefully accept the bread and then immediately give it to his or her hungry and starving child without taking a single bite. Parents are more than willing to continue their own terrible hunger so that their child may eat, truly loving their child more than themselves. This action gives true meaning to the commitment that exists between a parent and child and the proclaimed and committed-to part of the wedding vows that proclaim "until death do us part." This is a clear example of what we should strive to reach in our adult relationships.

Understanding this concept leads to the real challenge, which is whether we can love our chosen partner in life more than we love ourselves. Let me say that again. Can you love your partner in life more than you love yourself? Are you willing or even capable of reaching far beyond the 50/50 line in the sand to defy the conventional wisdom of give and take? Clearly of equal importance is whether your partner is willing and/or capable of loving you more than himself or herself. Are you capable of thinking outside the box? Failure to comprehend or get this concept or failure to exercise what it behooves us to do with this insight and understanding leads to repeated failed relationships and an emotionally isolated, empty, and lonely life experience.

To help add more clarity to this concept, I present two clinical vignettes for your consideration.

The first is the story of two young adults who are engaged to be married. The young man is a recent college graduate and his fiancée was still in school. The young man used to smoke pot so often and so much that it took him an extra two years to get his bachelor's degree. In fact, it was during his intensive outpatient rehab treatment that he met his wife-to-be. Her addiction problem was more serious than his as evidenced by the need for several hospitalizations and an extensive residential treatment experience. At this point in time she had been clean and sober for a little more than a year and had continued to regularly attend AA and NA meetings.

During one of our therapy sessions he was relating to me how much he cherished and loved her, how his new job indeed looked very promising, affording him the opportunity to take good care of her, an example being his ability to pay her tuition through graduation.

Knowing that he still smoked marijuana recreationally, restricting its use to the weekends now, I asked how his continuing to get high impacted his fiancée's recovery. He rather proudly responded to my question by noting that he loved and cared about her "so much" that he had discussed this activity on his part with her at great length, that he had been "open and honest" about this issue, that through being very "adult" about this issue he had gotten her permission to get high at home on the weekends. He felt that he had reached beyond the 50/50 thing in this particular instance.

My young patient was stunned that I totally disagreed with him. I pointed out that quite to the contrary he did not love his fiancée as much as he proclaimed or believed he did, as evidenced by his so-called "open and honest, adult" actions. I reminded him that he had previously reported to me that his fiancée's recovery was a life-or-death situation for her, that relapse was out of the question. Therefore, knowing this, the discussion about his getting high on the weekends in their apartment should never have been a consideration at all if he truly loved her and cared about her survival. I clarified that the fact that the discussion ever happened was evidence that he loved himself and his getting high more than he loved her! When he understood what I was saying, he responded with an explicative. When he had finally settled down, he said that my interpretation was a "real eye-opener." He made a commitment to work with me on the relationship with his fiancée in particular and relationships in general.

My second story focuses on a failure of the original parent-child relationship and how understanding the failure and putting it into perspective proved to be therapeutically helpful.

This vignette involves a seventeen-year-old patient of mine whose parents divorced when she was five years of age, leaving her to be raised by her mother and maternal grandparents. Her father was and is an alcoholic who has drifted in and out of her life over the years as he has similarly drifted from job to job. The patient was originally brought to me for evaluation and treatment as she complained of feeling depressed, this mood being associated with some suicidal ideation. She had also stopped going to school and as a consequence of her non-attendance had been withdrawn, where previously she had been an honor roll student. Regular therapy sessions and Prozac resulted in a return to her senior classes and honors grades. She was accepted to community college and had returned to her pre-morbid level of emotional functioning, possibly even a little better overall. However, despite her therapeutic gains, her relationship with her father remained problematic. It all came crashing down for her during the Christmas holidays.

With tears streaming down her cheeks and often choking on her words, she related to me that her father had shown up unannounced on Christmas day. She reported that she could smell a hint of alcohol on his breath when he hugged her and wished her a Merry Christmas. He gave her a card stating such, and almost as an aside or afterthought, he asked her to tell her grandfather, his father, that he had gotten her some really nice Christmas gifts. She was at first puzzled by this request but later found out that her paternal grandfather had given her father five hundred dollars to buy her Christmas presents! This was just one more in an endless series of disappointments and hurtful experiences she had lived through at the hands of her father. "Why? What have I done to deserve this?!" she sobbed.

Referring to my relational formula, I pointed out that it has always been the unfortunate reality that for whatever reasons, her father loved himself and his booze more than he was capable of loving her, that in truth this was in no way a reflection on her worth or lovability as a person, that her honors grades, her acceptance to college, her proven reliability at work, her honesty in relationships, her hopes and plans to someday help people through a career in nursing were in fact who she really was. I further clarified that her father would more than likely proclaim that he loved her if asked, but that his alcohol addiction and his overall lifestyle rendered him incapable of even minimally approaching a 50/50 relationship with her, much less ever being able to love her more than he loved himself, that it was his incapacity or inability to love and not any failing on her part. Conscious of the impact and power of a father's relationship with his daughter, I pointed out that clearly she was loved dearly by her mother, grandparents, and boyfriend. She responded well to this interpretive intervention. It helped her to understand and see that it truly was not a failing on her part, freeing her to start to move on emotionally. As with my other patient, there is still much work to do.

Ultimately, all of us should take a long hard look in the mirror at our true emotional selves. Are we involved in the delusional give-and-take type of relationship currently? Is there any real hope that the equation can change? If you really think about it, in a 50/50 relationship where each party only reaches out to the halfway point, each partner will learn or know little to nothing about the other person opposite them in the relationship, another reason why such relationships are so unfulfilling, empty, and so often ultimately fail. These flawed relationships often stagnate into an "if" and "when" expectation experience, where one or both parties hold back from really committing themselves while waiting for the day "when" their partner has finally proven their worth over time and only "if" they turn out to be what you expected them to be over time, fulfilling all your expectations. If you are currently involved in a give-and-take type of relationship, and if you are holding back on a full commitment waiting for the "when" and "if" to happen and there is little hope of this actually happening, maybe it's time to move on.

If two people with this insight and understanding can move to any degree to love each other more than they love themselves, then they may be able to reach and experience a level of emotional intimacy and love they would never have dreamed possible, truly "a shining city on the hill" for all to admire and seek.

Of course, you can always choose not to reach out as I have suggested or you may, in fact, be incapable of doing so without some therapeutic intervention. Sadly then, you will be left to essentially travel life's highway alone, keeping your most intimate personal thoughts, feelings, and needs to yourself, an overall empty and unfulfilling life journey. Tragically, it is my opinion that most of us are destined to travel life's highway in this manner. But it doesn't have to be this way! Remember? I'm the guy always thinking I'm going to find the pony. You can do it. You can make significant change in your relationships and live a more fulfilling life. It's never too late.

Don't be that dead fish that goes with the flow! I hope I've at least given to you some of the psychological tools to start. The clock is ticking. Don't procrastinate! Swim against the current of conventional wisdom. Make some waves!

But even if your fate is to travel life's highway alone and not make any waves or swim against the current, you may at the very least have gotten a better psychological self-understanding from this reading, and you can always still employ positive, self-initiated thought insertion if nothing else—my gift to you.

Once again, as with the first five chapters, there is so much more to be discussed and so much more to be understood, but that's for another time, another place or format, or maybe even another book.

Addendum 2
ADD/ADHD Medications, the Truth

Toward the end of chapter 4 I mentioned that I would try to clarify the best medication treatment regimen or intervention for each and every person suffering with ADD/ADHD, child, adolescent, or adult. This discussion is geared more specifically toward professionals who treat ADD/ADHD; people who believe that they have or are already in treatment for ADD/ADHD; people who have a loved one, relative, or friend with ADD/ADHD; and those who just want to be in the know. Since this is an area of special interest and psychiatric specialty for me, I would like to share the following information with you.

For more than half a century the tried and true medications have been methylphenidate (Ritalin) and amphetamine (Dexedrine/Adderall). Both drugs were introduced to the American market in 1950. Hundreds of millions of people have been treated with various forms and dosages of these drugs for the intervening half a century or more. There is clearly some comfort to be taken from this longevity of prescription. With the recent recall of so many drugs by the FDA due to adverse events or side effects, doesn't it make sense that after sixty years and close to a billion people treated, if there was something even remotely or seriously wrong with methylphenidate or amphetamine, it would have been discovered by now? Certainly CNN would have presented an exposé by now if there was anything negative even remotely reportable!

As a psychiatrist my career-long philosophy and approach to the care of all people has been to treat all my patients as if they were my own children or, now in my older years, my grandchildren or close family members. If I wouldn't prescribe a drug for my own child, grandchild, or close family member, why would I prescribe such for someone else's child or family member? Frankly, I am often taken aback by the prescription of so many different psychiatric drugs and different and often extreme dosages to an individual child or adult as it is. I am certainly not against the concept or implementation of "polypharmacy" when absolutely necessary, but I also strongly believe that with proper diagnosis, it is very often possible to apply the "KISS" principle: "Keep It Simple Stupid." However, a more intense and detailed discussion related to this area of practice is not relevant to the current discussion.

So, back to what medication is best for each individual with ADD/ADHD person. The answer can be found in the published genetic work of Dr. Stephen Faraone (2005) and the meta-analysis of Dr. L. Gene Arnold (2000). Note that of the first seven genes elucidated, five affect dopamine levels, metabolism, or transmission, one effects norepinephrine, and the last one affects serotonin. Therefore, statistically and logically it makes sense that more people with ADD/ADHD will have some level of problem in their dopamine system. A small percentage would have a dysfunction in both systems and an even smaller percentage with only a norepinephrine system malfunction. Based on this scientific thinking, the best medication or medications would effect positive changes on the dopamine side of the equation. And guess what? Methylphenidate and amphetamine are both "dopaminergic" meaning they both affect dopamine func-

tion and, therefore, are overall good initial treatment choices. This correlates with Dr. Arnold's data published in 2000
demonstrating that between methylphenidate and amphetamine there is up to a 92 percent robust, excellent clinical
response to proper medication intervention, with fully half
of the properly diagnosed ADD/ADHD patients responding
equally to either medication.

The initially confounding result from Dr. Arnold's meta-
analysis as published in 2000 was a difference in the percent
of "preferential" or best responders. Dr. Arnold and his group
found that approximately 29 percent of the properly diagnosed ADD/ADHD patients responded preferentially or best
to amphetamine while about 17 percent responded preferentially or best to methylphenidate. The 12 percent differential
was clearly real and not a meta-analytic or statistical artifact,
but was scientifically unexplainable in 2000.

Not until years later with the progress made in clarifying
the genetic code of this syndrome was the reason for this
12 percent effectiveness differential elucidated. The culprit
was the SNAP-25 gene, one of the identified group of five
genes that affects dopamine function. As we know, genes encode the production of proteins, and the protein encoded by
SNAP-25 is an integral part of the pre-synaptic dopamine
neuron's membrane. This protein's function as part of that
membrane is to facilitate the release of dopamine into the
space between the pre-synaptic and post-synaptic neurons,
a process essential to normal brain function. Therefore without SNAP-25 and its encoded protein, there is a resultant in-
hibition of and a resultant decreased dopamine release, resulting in decreased dopamine molecules being available for
neuron-to-neuron communication and function, ultimately
resulting in varying degrees of dysfunction or "deficit" within the dopamine system. This deficit results in the problems
with inattention and the many symptoms and signs of ADD/
ADHD.

Researchers have genetically engineered a non-SNAP-25
mouse, the "Coloboma" mouse, to demonstrate the results of
this genetic deletion, and I would invite you to look up more

information concerning this little brown fellow. Simply put, this genetically engineered little brown mouse explained the 12 percent differential in the number of preferential or best responders in favor of amphetamine prescription.

Functionally speaking, methylphenidate increases available dopamine by blocking the recycling or reuptake of available dopamine. Amphetamine, while also blocking recycling, also stimulates release of dopamine.

To simplify this concept I want you to think about a bathtub. When things are running normally, the tap is running at a good rate, with the input rate equally matched by the water that is flowing out through the drain, so the level of water in the tub remains basically constant. The constant level of water into and out of the tub equals normal attentional functioning.

In the case of ADD/ADHD the residual level of water in the tub is too low. This less-than-adequate level of water in the tub could be present as the result of either the tap running too slowly or the drain being open too wide.

Methylphenidate (Ritalin) works by plugging up the drain to a greater or lesser degree depending on the dose, the sought after end result being the level of water rising in the tub. Amphetamine has the dual action of plugging up the drain but also turning up the tap flow.

Therefore, without SNAP-25 and its encoded protein, dopamine levels are below normal secondary to decreased dopamine release or the tap running too slowly, and as a result of this, intervention with methylphenidate logically, and in practice, is relatively ineffective in these particular individuals. Clinically, in this situation methylphenidate is basically ineffective as it has very limited impact (if any at all) on dopamine release or turning up the tap, the problem that exists in the absence of the SNAP-25 gene. However, amphetamine does create a positive response as a direct result of its dual action. This thesis was borne out when the hyperactive Coloboma mice were fed methylphenidate and showed little to no improvement but clearly demonstrated improvement when fed amphetamine.

Therefore, if you want to cast a pharmacologic net to catch the most people with ADD/ADHD on the first attempt, scientific evidence would suggest the amphetamine molecule should be tried first, understanding that the methylphenidate net will also capture and help a very large group of people with ADD/ADHD.

Since it was established in 1950 that methylphenidate and amphetamine, when properly prescribed, were safe and effective, there remained two challenges. Since both methylphenidate and amphetamine had relatively similar "half" lives of about four hours, and knowing that ADD/ADHD is a 24/7/365 condition, it was paramount that longer-acting formulations had to be found and developed. The second challenge was overuse, misuse, abuse, and diversion of these compounds as they are both in the stimulant category of medications—non-narcotic schedule II drugs.

It took more than half a century for effective longer-acting products to emerge. They are Concerta, Adderall XR, Focalin XR, Ritalin LA, Medidate CD, and Daytrana, all introduced to the market since the year 2000. All these products addressed to a lesser or greater degree the need for longer-acting medication formulations. However, clinical experience showed that in most cases none of the new longer-acting formulations were really effective for quite long enough. This resulted in the need for an additional dose of medication, an "augmentation" dose, in the afternoon or early evening, to a significant degree defeating the goal of true once-a-day dosing and increasing the risk of unwanted side effects, which often contributed to an uneven clinical pharmacologic response. The one exception was Daytrana, which was a skin patch trans-dermal delivery system. Unfortunately, a patch worn on a daily basis over time did tend to produce unwanted skin reactions.

Despite their differences, the newer longer-acting formulations all ultimately proved to be still abuse prone and easily divertible. The first attempt to address the abuse issue was atomoxetine (Strattera), which is a non-stimulant medication approved by the FDA for the treatment of ADD/ADHD in 2002. Unfortunately, its effectiveness did not statistically rival the stimulant class of drugs in the vast majority of the properly diagnosed ADD/ADHD patients.

Then in 2007 Vyvanse was introduced to more thoroughly address the abuse issue. But get this! The active ingredient in Vyvanse was good old, proven, reliable amphetamine! How could it be that amphetamine, like methylphenidate, which is so easily prone to abuse, could become essentially impossible to abuse? The answer was that Vyvanse had a unique delivery system that took advantage of the body's natural system of absorbing nutrition. In essence, some really smart biochemist figured out that you can attach an l-lysine molecule, a naturally occurring amino acid, to the amphetamine molecule, and the resultant couple was totally inactive from a stimulant standpoint.

So, you could snort the resultant white powder or dissolve it, in saline and "shoot up," and basically nothing would happen. Wow! A stimulant, schedule II drug that is essentially almost completely without abuse potential. The question that remained was if the coupled molecules are inactive and, therefore, cannot be abused, how can Vyvanse help ADD/ADHD patients? It's a matter of guts. I mean it, guts! Once the capsule is swallowed or opened and its contents dissolved in water, juice, or soda, and once it gets past the stomach, it starts its twelve- to thirteen-hour journey down the small intestine or "small gut," which I refer to as being not dissimilar from *Finding Nemo*, the little clown fish that swims among the tentacles of the sea anemone. I use this comparison because that's what the human small gut or small intestine looks like inside—hundreds of thousands of tentacles, or "villi" as they are called, and they're even white just like the sea anemone's tentacles. The point is that like the sea anemone absorbs all its nutrition through its tentacles, so do we as humans absorb all our nutrition through our tentacles or villi. So, as the amphetamine/l-lysine-coupled molecules take their twelve- to thirteen-hour journey down and through this forest of villi, they get absorbed by way of an active transport mechanism, and once inside a villus, the coupled molecule moves on into the mesenteric blood system, where the enzymes in the red blood cells actively separate the l-lysine from the amphetamine, freeing the amphetamine to go about its business. Is that cool or what?

Finally, an effective, basically nonabusable, non-divertible product, and possibly the longest acting of them all, that can from a short-term or long-term safety standpoint and potentially use significantly less total active medication to reach the same, if not even a superior therapeutic outcome! All this and it's approved by the FDA for the treatment of children, adolescents, and adults, and it will work up to fourteen hours or longer with a single dose, in most cases totally eliminating the need for an additional dose of medication in the afternoon or evening.

I like to think of Vyvanse as fulfilling the popular beer commercial's ad, "great taste, less filling." Vyvanse has a longer, smoother, overall more satisfying clinical response, which is "great." And you can achieve this with so much less total stimulant medication per day, potentially up to 70 percent less, which is "less filling" in terms of any possible stress it might cause to a person's body or bodily functions in the short term or possibly, even more importantly, in the long run.

A final thought before moving on. Understanding the genetics of ADD/ADHD helps us to see that the syndrome has no statistical or scientific relationship to intelligence or other major psychiatric syndromes. Also keep in mind that part of the genetic code affects serotonin, a discussion somewhat beyond the scope of this book but well understood by most psychiatrists—serotonin dysfunction being associated with anxiety, moodiness, irritability, aggression, and impulsivity, symptoms often seen with ADD/ADHD patients over time.

Without some kind of intervention, the long-term prognosis for people with ADD/ADHD is truly not good, as evidenced in many published studies, particularly those by Dr. Timothy Wilens, Associate Professor of Psychiatry, Harvard University Medical School, documenting many negative outcomes in areas like education, substance use disorders, career failures, and relationship failures. But with proper intervention, the sky's the limit! After four decades in practice, many of my former patients are now doctors, lawyers, business executives, engineers, and so much more, career alone is far from always being the measure of success! Beyond jobs or specific careers, they, as a group, are more functional and happy people overall.

So many of my "kids," as I like to refer to them, stop their medications when they've reached their life goals. This sheds some light on the question of when or if to stop medication. Parents often ask me, particularly after their child has had an excellent clinical response to medication, "Doctor, does this mean that my child will have to take medication for the rest of their life?"

My response to this important and legitimate question is that although there is rather clear-cut medical evidence that ADD/ADHD may be a lifelong condition, it tends to ameliorate over time, often associated with a significant decrease to total disappearance of the hyperactivity. Understanding that a good percentage of people with ADD/ADHD experience that their symptoms proceed unabated into their adult life. I am reminded of two of my "kids" in particular.

Just recently a young lady was discussing with me whether the time was approaching for her to stop her prescribed stimulant medication. She was soon to graduate from college with her bachelor of science degree in nursing and was deciding between two offered positions post graduation. They were in a neonatal intensive care unit or a hospital emergency room. Both positions were in areas of nursing that gave her a real emotional "rush," feeling that this was what she was "born to do."

The other was a young man who landed a job as an Internet programming engineer. The job was to create and monitor online games like WoW. "Doc, can you believe it? I'll be paid big bucks to do what I love to do anyway and would have done for free!"

I advised both of these young adults to discontinue their prescribed medication and call me if they perceived they were having any functional impairments or problems. They were both very self-aware of their ADD/ADHD and its impact on their day-to-day lives and function, as we had worked together on these issues for many years. I have not heard from either of them at the time of this writing.

One of the pitfalls for parents is that they cannot see or accept that their child might have ADD/ADHD because the child can spend hours and hours playing video games or other similar activities that they love to do. That's the point! My two patients had reached a point in their lives where they were going to be doing what they loved to do! It's human nature to love to do what we love to do! Duh! It's the activities that are most often required for our ultimate success in life, the "extra" that I discussed earlier, that we don't love or even like to do, like going to school or, God forbid, doing homework, that are the most compromised by ADD/ADHD.

The point is that ADD/ADHD negatively impacts "non-interested" learning activities, and non-interested learning, fortunately or unfortunately, is often essential for an individual to ultimately be successful in life.

Addendum 3
Face Theory and the Holy Land

Several years ago, I sent a letter to then Secretary General for the United Nations, Kofi Annan. This action was the result of long discussions with my Jewish friend and psychologist colleague Dr. Steven Waranch. Now, Steve and I have been good friends for more than twenty years, and his stated view on the conflict in the Middle East, particularly related to Israel, is understandably painted with a Zionist brush. However, Steve himself is not a radical person in any sense of the word or stretch of the imagination.

Being neither Jewish nor Muslim myself, I understandably saw this clearly difficult situation somewhat differently. It seemed to me that if the Torah or Old Testament was historically correct, then Moses and the Israelites, after forty years of wandering around in the wilderness, came upon the "Promised Land," the land of milk and honey, the land promised by Jehovah to the Jews. There was only one problem with this wonderful prophesized discovery. There were people already living in the so-called "Promised Land"! Claiming divinely bestowed right, Moses drove out by force the indigenous people who were living there. The now-exiled people obviously didn't like the situation even a little bit. Besides that, they didn't believe in the God of the Jews nor did they believe in the validity of the Torah. For the ensuing 3,000 years they have been trying to take back the land and drive out the Israelites.

Nobody denies the intensity or the toll in property and lives that both sides have extracted from each other during this 3,000-year war. But, in a sense, the Palestinians and the Israelis are not unlike Cain and Able, in that they are essentially brothers from a genetic pool standpoint, their ancestry coming from identical or very similar sources.

After hours of discussion with Dr. Waranch over our favorite Chinese food, and after considerable contemplation on my own time, I came up with the following Tsaoism action plan.

I realize that President George W. Bush, as a hoped-for positive legacy for his embattled presidency, felt there was an outside chance for peace based on what he referred to as a democratic Palestinian state and an already democratic Jewish state. I hoped he was right! But, things overall haven't gone very well nor according to plan, as reported recently by various news outlets.

Maybe the problem needs to be assessed with a new and different set of eyes, Asian eyes! It seems to me that conventional wisdom and inside-the-box thinking has met with little success over the intervening centuries, the idea of an independent Jewish people and an independent Palestinian people living in close proximity with peace and harmony having been around for a long time. Therefore, regardless of the Bush legacy, my plan has two separate and distinct components.

First of all, I believe that we can all agree that the United Nations is headquartered and its buildings physically exist on the island of Manhattan in the city of New York. But, it's not in the United States! That's right, the land is international ground, in effect owned by no one, no country or other political entity, and yet owned by everyone, the world community.

So, part of my plan would be to apply the same principle to Jerusalem, turning the Holy City and a limited number of its surrounding suburbs into international ground, neither owned by the Israelis nor the Palestinians but owned by all, everyone!

Part two of my plan goes back to the face theory and its psychological emotional tagging. Since the Israelis and Palestinians are decedents of essentially the same genetic stock, they look alike and as a result, externally, for all intents and purposes, you cannot tell them apart visually. In fact, during the 3,000-plus-year conflict, each side has mistakenly killed many of its own because of this mistaken identity. This is of particular importance as history tells us that this centuries-long conflict has basically been a crusade, jihad, or holy war. Therefore, the international police force in my intended plan not only must not look like the people of the region, but they shouldn't have any historical "emotional baggage" calling for revenge of previous wrongs, real or perceived, nor should they give a flying whoop-de-do about the Jewish or Muslim faiths. This takes a lot of the bite out of this long-standing adversarial situation, which all along has been a "holy war." It also seems clear to me that previous efforts at intervention by Russia, France, Germany, England, and the United States have not been, by any stretch of imagination, successful because the "faces" of these nations look too much like those of the conflicting parties. In addition, these countries have religious or sociopolitical ties to one side or the other. This has been a major obstacle to establishing reasonable levels of trust on both sides of the dispute, without which a lasting peace cannot realistically ever be attained. The obvious answer is that the police force must be Asian and have "Asian faces."

Further developing my plan, the international Asian police force should come from many different Asian countries. The Koreas would be motivated to send troops, the South as in emerging world economic power; the North, now apparently agreeing to unilateral nuclear disarmament, hoping to improve its global political image and solve some of its domestic problems. With a joint collaborative effort over time, it might even improve relations between the North and the South. China's motive to send troops would also give the current Beijing regime an opportunity to improve its negative worldwide image by becoming involved in a peace-keeping effort, deflecting some of the criticism from its human rights transgressions, the Olympics, and obvious industrial pollution problems. Vietnam would be motivated for similar reasons, and with its emerging economy and tourist industry, it would like to show its stability and that it can now finally be a contributing participant in the world community. Finally, let the Japanese oversee and administrate the whole deal. The Japanese are proven excellent businessmen and their "carrot" could be a permanent seat on the United Nations Security Council, if they should succeed in doing a good job. They have really coveted a permanent seat for many years, and certainly establishing a lasting peace in the Middle East would deserve serious consideration for such a reward!

With the establishment of a truly safe and well-managed Jerusalem, religious pilgrims from around the world would be able to travel safely to, visit, and enjoy all of the thirty-five most hallowed sites for the three major religious factions. Tourism would skyrocket! Taxes on hotel rooms, restaurants, and souvenirs would follow suit and could be used to defray, or even totally cover, the cost of the United Nations' international peace-keeping force, a clear-cut win-win situation! With the passage of time and the passing of generations, some of the old wounds would hopefully heal or be lost to personal memory, leading to real and lasting peace. This goes against the biblical story of Solomon's wisdom when he suggested cutting the baby in half; in this case the baby remains whole and neither of the conflicting parties gets the baby! Instead, all of us in the world community do!

If you're wondering what response I got from the Secretary General of the United Nations, I didn't! At least some staffer from Senator John Warner's office sent me a note thanking me for my "thoughts." That was nice! But the senatorial response more or less implied, "Don't call us. We'll call you." I never got a call! Maybe I'll hear from Ban Ki-moon, the current secretary general, since he and I both share Asian faces!

Of course, working out the details in terms of logistics, diplomacy, and politics, I cede that task and responsibility to the current world leaders and brains much bigger than mine. It would be my hope that they won't revert back to just jumping up and down, beating their chests, and making threatening sounds in the Neanderthal style that they have demonstrated all too readily and frequently in the past!

Final Thoughts

This brings to a conclusion my observations and Tsaoist sugges- tions for now. I really appreciate your time and effort invested in reading and, hopefully, your tolerance of my thoughts, sugges- tions, and ramblings. After all, it was my intention that this endeav- or would flow more like a conversation between old friends rather than a formal lecture. Like my therapeutic experience with Eddie, even though I was his psychiatrist, sharing a stretch of the highway of life with him certainly also enriched my life immeasurably. I hope that reading and sharing my thoughts and recommendations about stretches of your life's highway may in some small way change and enrich your life experience too.

It's been nice having this conversation. I hope I'll get a chance to converse with you again at some time in the not-too-distant future, possibly even face-to-face. That would be nice. I'd really love to hear some of your observations and thoughts. At the very least, make the commitment not to be the leaf in the stream or that dead fish!

Sincerely,

Doc